PRAIRIE WISDOM

Reflections on Life in the Dakotas

MICHAEL J. COYNER

ABINGDON PRESS / Nashville

PRAIRIE WISDOM
REFLECTIONS ON LIFE IN THE DAKOTAS

This book is printed on acid-free paper.

Library of Congress Cataloging-in-Publication Data

Coyner, Michael J.
    Prairie wisdom: reflections on life in the Dakotas/by Michael J.
Coyner.
        p. cm.
    ISBN 0-687-09051-2 (acid-free paper)
    1. Christian life—United Methodist authors. 2. Coyner,
Michael J.—Journeys—Dakota Territory. 3. Dakota Territory—
Description and travel. I. Title.

BV4501.2.C686 1999
287'.6'092—dc21
[B]
                                                            99-057364

00 01 02 03 04 05 06 07 08 09—10 9 8 7 6 5 4 3 2 1

MANUFACTURED IN THE UNITED STATES OF AMERICA

CONTENTS

Introduction: Moving to the Dakotas / 5

The People and the Land / 9

Surviving the First Winter / 15

Consider the Sunflowers / 19

For the Forgiveness of Sins and Vandals / 22

Pavement Ends / 26

Christmas in a Box / 29

Light in the Darkness / 33

A Better Use of Sandbags / 36

Pastors Are Human, Too / 39

Sap on the Family Tree / 44

Connected by the Inner Net / 47

Thanks El Niño / 50

Cloning Naomi / 54

Shaved Heads / 58

Noticing One Another / 61

Too Much Vitamin "I" Is Bad for Our Health / 65

Good-bye, Bandit / 69

Horsing Around the Badlands / 73

What Am I Selling? / 77

Kissing Pigs / 82

Don't Forget First Base / 85

When Is a Christian? / 89

No More Violence / 93

Uffda! / 96

The First Snow / 99

Have a Seat / 103

Lessons From the Grinch / 106

Check This Out / 109

Remote-Starting the Church / 113

Celebrating Small Successes / 117

Rebuilding Faith / 120

Sundogs and Other Signs / 124

The Prisoner's Mite / 127

Prayed For / 130

Lost and Found / 133

Spiritual? / 137

Getting the Family Together / 141

Turbulence / 145

Looking Through the Windshield / 149

Lessons From a Kildeer / 152

O Canada! / 155

Finding Faith / 158

INTRODUCTION

Moving to the Dakotas

---

*A*fter my election as a bishop in 1996 and my assignment to the Dakotas Area (which includes the two states of North Dakota and South Dakota), my wife Marsha and I prepared to move to Fargo. Neither of us had ever set foot in either state until our visit in early August of 1996 to see the area and to meet the Cabinet and others with whom we would be living and working. It was a feeling of "adventure" for us as we prepared to leave Indiana and move to the Fargo area.

Such transitions are never easy, and there is a litany that I have used in every new appointment where I have moved from or to. It goes like this:

The winds blow, the world changes, the way is uncertain. And God says, "Keep moving, for you are a Pilgrim People."

We pray for security, but God terrifies us with freedom.

We pray for a temple that stands, but God gives us tents that move.

We want easy answers, but God gives us the cries of others in need.

We want conclusions, but God gives us beginnings.

The winds blow, the world changes, and the way is uncertain. Is there nothing that endures?

Only the steadfast love of the One who created the universe and who sustains us in his love.

This litany sustains me, as it reminds me that God goes with me—or rather that I am called to go with God in every move I make. It helps me remember that God is the source of our sense of "home" and that God is the One who sustains us through the transitions of life.

I received a lovely letter about this litany from a woman I knew in my first appointment after seminary. Marietta wrote to tell me about her husband's illness, their move into a nursing home facility, and the difficult transitions of their lives. She even wrote, "Old age stinks!"

Marietta went on to describe how this litany has helped her with the tough transitions of old age and moving out of their home of many years. She also has shared that litany with other residents who are dealing with transitions, especially the death of a spouse. Marietta wrote to tell me how much this litany has meant to her and to others.

The move to Fargo, North Dakota, was a transition, a change, and an adventure. Perhaps the most difficult aspect of the move was that Marsha and I also became "empty-nesters" for the first time, since we left our college-age son behind in Indiana and our daughter had already graduated and moved to Virginia for her job with General Electric.

So here we were, in a new land, with new people, without any children at home, adjusting to the idea of being a "bishop" and spouse, and wondering what this transition would mean.

What did we find in this transition? We found what we always find: God is good, God leads us through change, God's people are similar everywhere, and somehow God's presence is best known as we face change and transition with an attitude that asks, "God, what would you have us to learn from this?"

I began writing these "Life in the Dakotas" reflections as a way of dealing with these transitions myself and of sharing with others (especially family and friends back in Indiana, plus new friends in the Dakotas) what the transition to the Dakotas was like for me. The "Life in the Dakotas" reflections began as e-mail devotionals that I sent out more-or-less weekly to pastors and churches in the Dakotas who are on-line, with copies to family and friends and to other bishops. The series has grown from there, with my e-mail list expanding to over six hundred persons, many of whom forward these reflections on to others. My sister Jill, for example, works for Rockwell Industries in Chicago; and she forwards "Life in the Dakotas" to several of her co-workers and staff. Several bishops have copied certain issues of "Life in the Dakotas" to their entire conferences to address a specific issue.

Who would have known that God could use a transition time in my life to provide a conduit for sharing, reflections, and prayers to so many people? Yet that is the message of the litany: "Keep moving, for you are a Pilgrim People."

THE PEOPLE AND THE LAND

―――――

O give thanks to the LORD, *for he is good;*
for his steadfast love endures forever.
Let the redeemed of the LORD *say so,*
those he redeemed from trouble
and gathered in from the lands,
from the east and from the west,
from the north and from the south.
(Psalm 107:1-3)

―――――

One of the first comments made to me after moving to the Dakotas was, "We are geographically challenged." I have learned this truth as I have traveled the many miles of the Dakotas Area—North and South Dakota—a total of 150,000 square miles. The population of the two states has finally grown back to its pre-depression and dust bowl level (about 700,000 in South Dakota and 600,000 in North Dakota), but our cities are two to three times the size in the 1990's that they were in the 1920's. Thus, our rural areas are very sparsely populated, and many small towns are simply disappearing. It

―――――

also means that everyone in the Dakotas is aware of the immense size of the land and the incredible distances between population centers.

In the Dakotas we are geographically challenged, but we are also geographically blessed.

The land is large and it is varied. The eastern sections of both states, and especially of North Dakota, give a whole new meaning to the word "flat." This flat area is the Red River Valley, formerly prehistoric Lake Agassiz, and the flat land is the reason for the spring floods—the water has no where to go, at least not in any hurry.

Moving west and south out of the valley, the land quickly becomes rolling prairie. There are countless "sloughs" (pronounced "slews") that contain too much water in the wet seasons and too little in the dry. Varieties of wildlife and wildflowers prevail, and these endure the harsh winters in amazing fashion. I have seen pheasants, deer, one bald eagle, antelope, buffalo, and more rabbits than one could count. The rolling prairie is farmed and ranched, but it is reluctant to be tamed.

The greatest change in the land occurs as one moves westward across the Missouri River. The change is immediate, as the land moves from rolling prairie farmland to a more "western" looking open range of ranches and ultimately to the Bad Lands (one set in each state) and the Black Hills of southwestern South Dakota. This divide leads to much discussion about "west river" and "east river" issues, and many have noted that the Dakotas should have been divided into East and West, rather than the arbitrary North and South. The Missouri River (sometimes called "Big Water" in North Dakota) has a dominating and dividing influence on the land—and upon the people. The most obvious difference is that east river farmers tend to wear seed corn caps and west river ranchers tend to wear cowboy hats.

The people of the Dakotas are much more diverse than I first realized or expected. At first it seems that most are Norwegian or German, and it also seems that we have "more Lutherans than people" here. I have also met a variety of Ukranians, German Russians, Swedes, and even some Irish and English.

The German Russians are the most segmented of the population groups, and their history explains the reason. They were Germans who had been brought to Russia to populate the land, and who were later forced out. In Russia they had maintained their German heritage and traditions, and after leaving they discovered that Germany was not the same country they had left. It was as if they had kept their own German heritage in suspended animation, while Germans at home had continued to change and modernize. As a last resort, many of these German Russians came to America and settled in the Dakotas as the last place where land was available. Still today they congregate in the central part of the Dakotas, just north and south of the state line.

The most invisible people in the Dakotas are the Native Americans. In fact, many "white" people seem to pretend that the Dakotas, Lakotas, Nakotas, and other tribal groups are not still around. Of course, many of these same white people are glad to go to the many casinos on Indian land; but they seem to believe that Native Americans only exist in old Western movies. Our ministries with Native Americans here in the Dakotas are limited, and any new efforts are met with a suspicion that is warranted by the many, many lies and failures of white people in the past.

Those Native Americans (some of whom prefer to be called American Indians) who live on the "res"— the reservations—are among the poorest of the population groups in the Dakotas. Their land tends to be poor for farming, the government agencies have created a terrible dependency, the churches have not done well in meeting their needs, and the destructive power of alcohol has devastated their home life and their self-esteem. We United Methodists struggle to know how to be in ministry with our Native American brothers and sisters in the Dakotas, and I have to admit that many persons would prefer to pretend that these Native peoples do not really exist.

All of the people in the Dakotas are geographically challenged and geographically blessed. People live miles and miles apart. One young pastoral family told me that they live in a remote area, meaning, "We are eighty miles from a McDonald's." This distance is always an issue for people in the Dakotas—we have to plan travel time in a way that I never thought about in Indiana.

Yet, this distance seems to bring people closer together. People here love to get together, and meetings are always social occasions. People stay in one another's home as they travel in these two states, partly as a necessity because of the lack of motels in some places, but mostly as a preference. People enjoy staying and visiting with one another. Conference meetings are less frequent here, but the meetings always last longer. After all, when you drive five hundred miles to a meeting, you don't just stay for an hour.

Perhaps it is also the distance that makes people here so honest and direct. I find that conversation in the Dakotas is refreshingly frank, with very little tap dancing around issues. Folks just say what they think, even if you aren't asking for their opinion. During my get-acquainted times that first fall, I asked open-ended questions like, "What do you need from me as your bishop?" This led to responses such as, "Well, what can you do?" or "Just leave us alone." After preaching in one of our churches and being warmly received, one older woman came through the receiving line, looked at me carefully, and said, "You don't look nearly as young up close as you did from a distance."

Looking at one another from a distance is part of life here in the Dakotas. We use E-mail and telephones and even regular mail to stay in touch. But the land, the immense and open land, always reminds us that we are separated, too.

I am grateful to be a part of a "connectional church" that helps to bring people together and to hold people together here in the Dakotas.

And I pray:

O GOD,
Bette Midler sang that you look at us "From a Distance,"
And the distance seems wide as it keeps us apart.
But your grace brings us close to each other,
And even closer to your loving heart.

Over the miles and miles of this land that we love
Where deer and buffalo really do roam,
Bring us ever closer to one another,
And remind us we are never alone.

For it is only your presence in this land, the Dakotas,
Filling each one of our homes,
That gives us a sense of belonging,
From knowing we are yours alone.

AMEN.

SURVIVING THE FIRST WINTER

———

If it had not been the LORD who was on our side . . .

then the flood would have swept us away,

the torrent would have gone over us;

then over us would have gone the raging waters.

(Psalm 124:1, 4-5)

After moving to Fargo, North Dakota, in the fall of 1996, we knew that winter was coming soon. Nearly everyone we met those early months was friendly, and nearly everyone told us "horror stories" about their worst winters here. Some seemed to want to warn us about the severity of this land and its harsh winters, and many of those persons even gave us tips on keeping a "survival kit" in the trunk of the car. Others seemed to be teasing us, not really expecting us to encounter a harsh winter during our time here in the Dakotas.

The fall of 1996 started out beautifully, and we did not even see any snow until mid-November. But once the winter of 1996–97 arrived, it stayed . . . and stayed . . . and stayed. Suddenly we began to

———

receive phone calls from some of the very same people who had warned us about winters in the Dakotas. Most of those calls were to apologize for this bad winter, as if they could actually do anything about the weather! Most of the time, we found the winter to be enjoyable, with the blizzards (nearly every week for a while) giving us some time for staying at home, reading, sending E-mails, and enjoying the quiet. Sometimes the winter got to be boring, repetitious, with every new blizzard seeming to be more of the same. As we approached the record for snowfall in Fargo, I found myself hoping that we would break the record, because when you are having a tough winter you might as well have a sense of achievement about enduring the thing.

Somewhere I read that Native Americans had up to fourteen different words for the reality that we call snow—with some of their words meaning "snow that is piled high" or "snow that drifts around the trees" or other such descriptive terms. After surviving the winter of 1996–97, I believe that we need more words in our language for snow, because I saw snow here in the Dakotas that I had never seen before, snow that defies description, snow that is not fully labeled by the simple word *snow*.

But we survived those 119 inches of snow in Fargo and the eight or ten blizzards. My wife Marsha and I went away to Florida for a spring vacation in late March, returned home on April 2 to find most of the snow melted, and felt good about surviving our first winter in the Dakotas.

Then came The Flood. It deserves capital letters, because it was a five-hundred-year flood. One last blizzard of extremely wet snow hit in early April and added to the incredible snowmelt and water content. The Flood began. We actually ended up having to sandbag around our neighborhood because of snowmelt from all of the farmland that had been covered with huge amounts of snow all winter. Fargo survived The Flood, but Grand Forks did not.

Flying over Grand Forks in a small airplane, seeing the incredible amount of water, knowing that months and years would be required to rebuild and restore that area was just about the most incredible sight and experience of my life. Fifty thousand people were suddenly homeless, and the fact that no one died during the Grand Forks evacuation is truly amazing. The town seemed like a ghost town during my first few trips there after the water receded. Being with the Grand Forks people, preaching in both of our churches there, and seeing the faith and courage of the people are memories that will stay with me long after the last home is demolished or cleaned up.

Spring and summer finally came, the land was carpeted with beautifully changing colors of crops and wildflowers. Reminders of winter and The Flood began fading away. Summer in the Dakotas is a time of respite, a time of remembering the harshness of last year's winter and a time of talking furtively about the upcoming winter. People in the Dakotas never really let go of winter. They are always remembering last year and fearing the next winter. Some people cannot seem even to enjoy summer, because it is, for them, just a break between one winter and the next.

Life goes on in the Dakotas. Signs of God's goodness abound. Evidence of people's generosity and caring for one another is evident everywhere. The generous response of our United Methodist churches (within the Dakotas and outside) continues to grow. One national relief person said to me, "Churches that were basically good, strong churches before the disaster will be strengthened by it; but churches that had divisions or problems before the disaster will find those problems magnified by the disaster." He was right, not just about churches but also about people. Disaster makes some people stronger, their faith more lively. Disaster for others is truly a disaster. What makes the difference? It seems to be a matter of perspective. Living in the Dakotas has given me a new perspective on many things and leads me to pray:

O Lord,
God of the mountains, God of the plains,
God of the blizzards, God of the rains,
Pour out your mercy, your abundance of grace,
Give me the strength for this new place.

Help me to pray, help me to preach,
Help me to guide, help me to teach.
Give me the wisdom, the discernment I need,
Give me the courage to know how to lead.

Thanks for these people, thanks for this land,
Thanks for your presence, holding my hand.
This is the place you want me to be,
Give me the vision to see what you see.

Amen.

CONSIDER THE SUNFLOWERS

Consider the lilies of the field; how they grow; they neither toil nor spin, yet I tell you, even Solomon in all his glory was not clothed like one of these.

(Matthew 6:28-29)

*J*esus told his disciples (when they were worrying too much about their own needs and their own future): "Consider the lilies of the field." I have seen the wildflowers in the Holy Land of Israel and Jordan, and they are beautiful. I can imagine Jesus pointing to the beautiful colors of the flowers on a hillside near the Sea of Galilee and saying, "Consider the lilies."

Here in the Dakotas, Jesus would say, "Consider the sunflowers." There is nothing quite as beautiful as a field of sunflowers on a mid-August day in the Dakotas. It is possible to drive by miles and miles of these huge yellow beauties—and to sense a splendor that no fancy clothing can match.

Sunflowers are big business in the Dakotas, a wonderful cash crop. The largest sunflower processing plants in the world are located here. Some sunflowers are grown for their oil, while others are grown for their edible seeds. Sunflowers are also a durable crop, able to grow in this tough climate. I have seen farmers harvesting sunflowers in fields that already are covered with snow—as long as the valuable sunflower head is not snowed under, the crop can still be harvested. Where corn or beans might succumb to the harsh weather, sunflowers often stand tall and healthy.

But sunflowers are more about beauty than about money. They grow to great heights (seven feet or more). They seem to turn toward the sun (I am not sure that this is true in any biological sense, but they appear to turn and follow the sun's course during each day). And once they are fully matured, they bow their heads as if reverently giving thanks to God.

We can learn a lot about life if we consider the sunflowers. We can learn about toughness in the midst of harsh times. We can learn about turning our faces toward the light of God. We can learn about bowing our heads in thanksgiving to God when our life bears fruit. We can learn about providing beauty to the world.

Most of all, we can learn from sunflowers about trusting God. Although sunflowers may not be conscious of their daily problems in the way that we are as human beings, sunflowers do remind us simply to grow and blossom where we are planted, to rely upon God who provides for our needs, and to provide beauty and substance to our world. Maybe a little less worry and a lot more trust would help us, too. Maybe we need to be take ourselves and our ministry less seriously, and we need simply to enjoy the beauty of the world that God has provided. Maybe the church is called to feed our people, but we also need to give our people beauty and a sense of trust in God's goodness.

Consider the sunflowers of the field. As Jesus said, "If God so clothes the grass of the field, which is alive today and tomorrow is thrown into the oven [or the harvester], will he not much more clothe you—you of little faith? Therefore do not worry, saying, 'What will we eat?' or 'What will we drink?' or 'What will we wear?' . . . But strive first for the kingdom of God and his righteousness, and all these things will be given to you as well. So do not worry about tomorrow, for tomorrow will bring worries of its own. Today's trouble is enough for today" (Matthew 6:30-34).

I consider the sunflowers of the field, and I pray:

O LORD,

Thank you for such beauty in this wide open land, showing your precious care, the glory of your creative hand.

Thank you for your sunshine that is reflected from above by sunflowers and other bright flowers of your love.

May the sunflowers teach us to stand tall and firmly in place, when we are surrounded by troubles and in need of your grace.

Let the sunflowers witness about standing strong and straight no matter what the circumstances or how long we must wait.

May all of our lives be such a reflection of your grace. May our faith shine like flowers in each and every place.

May our faith be strong and straight and true. May we also reflect the sunshine that comes from you.

AMEN.

FOR THE
FORGIVENESS OF
SINS AND VANDALS

Then Peter came and said to him, "Lord, if another member of the church sins against me, how often should I forgive? As many as seven times?" Jesus said to him, "Not seven times, but, I tell you, seventy-seven times."

(Matthew 18:21-22)

On a beautiful sunny Sunday afternoon in October, the Calvary United Methodist Church in Fargo was vandalized by four young boys. A thirteen-year-old was the ringleader, and the other three were third graders. They got into the church through an open window and spent about two hours spray-painting terrible graffiti around the church, throwing trash, turning over furniture, wrecking the children's rooms, removing and desecrating the Communion table, overturning the pulpit, and causing a great deal of other damage.

The pastor arrived for Sunday evening activities and interrupted their spree. He caught one of the boys and quickly learned the identities of all four vandals. The police arrived and made the boys and their parents view all the destruction. The oldest

------

boy continued to laugh and to brag, "We were really cookin' in here!"

The congregation and the entire Fargo community were shocked by such an act of violence, scorn, and desecration of one of our church buildings. However, I have been impressed by the caring and forgiving attitude of the pastor and the people of Calvary church.

As I toured the church on Monday morning with the pastor, the district superintendent, and several of the laity of the church, I found myself becoming tearful to see how innocent religious facilities and decorations had been so deliberately devastated. Three scenes from the vandalized church affected me deeply.

One of the men of the church (a trustee, I believe) said to me quietly, "We must be doing something right." I thought for a moment that I had misheard him, but then I realized the truth of what he was saying. Whenever a church (or a person) is involved in doing the work of Christ, there does seem to come the opposition of evil.

To put it another way: perhaps the worst thing that can be said about most of us and our churches is that we are ignored by society, not opposed or criticized. That is why Jesus said, "Blessed are you when people revile you and persecute you . . . on my account" (Matthew 5:11). Although I feel sad and angry about those misguided boys who trashed the church, they were probably acting out a real hostility in our culture against active and transformational churches.

A second image comes from the nursery. In the midst of the trash and filth, I found a picture of Jesus with the face spray-painted red. I am sure that the wet paint covered Jesus' face, but as the

paint dried the face of Christ was re-emerging!
What a powerful image! We prefer to see Christ in
his powerful Easter triumph, able to meet our
every need. That damaged picture reminded me
that Christ is often seen in our culture as one
bloodied, attacked, and scorned. Yet the face of
Christ emerges, ready to heal and forgive.

The third image was a beautiful banner for
World Communion Sunday that still hung in its
place over the mess in the sanctuary. With pictures
of the cup and the grapes of Communion, it simply
proclaimed, "For the forgiveness of sins." What a
contrast to see that peaceful and powerful message
in a sanctuary so recently filled with wanton
destruction. That message was echoed repeatedly
by the pastor and people of the church who said,
"We feel so sorry for those boys; to be so young and
so filled with hatred. What will become of them?
How can we help them?"

I weep as I think of how easily someone could
damage the things of faith that I love. I weep as I
think of those four boys, so angry and so misled. I
weep when I think of the forgiveness and patience
shown by the people of Calvary church. And I weep
as I realize the depth of love that must be required
for God to keep on forgiving and healing all of us.

And so I pray:

O LORD,

*How sad it is to see your church vandalized by
those who neither understand nor care about the
gospel we try to proclaim or the love and forgiveness
that we share.*

But how much more sad you must be to see your church when it is irrelevant and ignored; when its ministry seems ineffective and weak and it is unable to proclaim and serve its Lord.

Protect our churches and our people, O God. Protect us from vandals who seek to deface; but protect us even more from irrelevance and inability to proclaim your good grace.

AMEN.

Pavement Ends

Not that I have already obtained this or have already reached the goal; but I press on to make it my own, because Christ Jesus has made me his own. Beloved, I do not consider that I have made it my own; but this one thing I do: forgetting what lies behind and straining forward to what lies ahead, I press on toward the goal for the prize of the heavenly call of God in Christ Jesus.

(Philippians 3:12-14)

One of the most prevalent highway warning signs in the Dakotas these days is the one that says "Pavement Ends." Many of our roads that have been under water are now being rebuilt. Oftentimes this means that you are driving along a perfectly fine road, when suddenly you see this warning sign, and then you find yourself driving on gravel, dirt, or mud.

I have driven into such conditions on Interstate 94 west of Valley City, North Dakota; on US 12 east of Webster, South Dakota; on US 81 west of Madison, South Dakota; and on countless state highways and county roads. The worst of all of these "pavement ends" situations is around Devil's Lake, North Dakota. That lake is twenty feet higher than it was ten years ago, and it has grown from 60,000 acres to over 140,000 acres. All this is due to the rising water table that continues to flood so much of the prairie and plains of the Dakotas. Many of our roads were built years ago in areas that were dry but that now are quite wet. Thus we have road construction and road rebuilding all over the Dakotas, as the various highway repair teams work to raise the level of the roadbed above that of the surrounding wet areas.

It can be quite disconcerting to be driving along on a paved road and suddenly encounter a "pavement ends" sign.

Life is like that, too. Things can be going quite smoothly in life, when suddenly the "pavement ends" and you find yourself in a very rough part of the journey. Maybe you get an unexpected diagnosis from the doctor. Or your spouse leaves you. Or the Staff-Parish Relations Committee informs you that they are requesting a change of pastors. Or your company decides to "downsize" (a term that I detest) and you find yourself out of a job after many years of faithful service. Or maybe your understanding of yourself is suddenly challenged. Or your children disappoint you. Or a loved one dies. Life can be going along very smoothly, when you suddenly encounter a time when the "pavement ends" and the trip becomes rough.

At such moments, it really helps to have a Pathfinder to help lead you through these rough stretches. I recently was driving in a rainstorm; the wind was blowing, and visibility was fading as evening approached. Suddenly the car in front of me flashed his lights to warn me. I saw the sign "Pavement Ends," and the road became unsteady and dangerous. It was a great comfort to be able to follow that local driver as he led me through the rough stretch of road.

The Letter to the Hebrews reminds us that we have such a Pathfinder in life, Jesus Christ, who is the "pioneer and perfecter of our faith" (12:2). Christ has already endured everything that we might encounter in life: suffering, aloneness, being deserted by friends, opposition, grief over loved ones, and death. No matter how rough a stretch of road we may encounter in life, Christ has traveled that way before us. Now he is there to lead us and to help us through those times when the "pavement ends." Paul's letter to the Philippians also talks about trusting Christ for the journey, and he calls us to "press on" toward the goal of our faith journey.

I press on in faith, and I pray:

———

O GOD,
Lead us forward in faith,
Keep us safely in your will.
May we discover your presence
Guiding us and leading us still.

When it seems the pavement ends,
When it seems that the road is rough,
Lead us on with your grace and goodness,
And give us a faith that is tough.

Christ goes on before us,
Leading us along the way;
Help us to follow his guidance
And to travel with him today.

AMEN.

———

CHRISTMAS IN A BOX

When the fullness of time had come, God sent his Son, born of a woman, born under the law, in order to redeem those who were under the law, so that we might receive adoption as children. (Galatians 4:4)

Sometimes Christmas really does come in a box. Most of the flood victims in Grand Forks in 1997 lost everything they had stored in their basements, including their Christmas lights and decorations. Of course most of those same people did not immediately replace those Christmas items as they cleaned up their homes from the mud and filth of the flood.

Suddenly the Christmas season was approaching, and hundreds of homes in the Grand Forks area did not have any Christmas decorations. The answer? Christmas boxes. Through our Upper Midwest Recovery (UMR) we received and prepared hundreds of boxes of Christmas ornaments, lights, and decorations. These items were put into watertight plastic containers (the 15 gallon size) and transported to Grand Forks, where they were distributed to any-

---

one needing Christmas decorations. Each kit was valued at $75 to $100, and our volunteers in the UMR warehouse made sure that only new and nice decorations were included. The Wesley United Methodist Church in Grand Forks got heavily involved in this project and distributed over ninety of these boxes themselves. Their newsletter described the results: "As we hand out these watertight boxes of Christmas decorations, we see first the smiles, and then the tears of joy and gratitude for these generous gifts." Their newsletter continued, "All this generous outpouring of compassion and care has been overwhelming. In the midst of feeling so unworthy, how does one begin to say thank you enough to everyone? We did nothing to deserve it. Others just recognized our need and responded with who they were and what they had. . . . Christmas is a reminder of God's outpouring love to us. We are grateful for the Christ in others who offer themselves to us."

One of the humorous sidelights of this project was the difficulty of finding and purchasing enough of these watertight containers. My wife Marsha went with Nina Martin, our Upper Midwest Recovery director, on several shopping trips to the local stores in Fargo. They created quite a stir as they lugged dozens of these containers through the check-out lines. They reported that this led to lots of interesting conversations as clerks and other customers asked what they were doing with so many large plastic containers—and they had a chance to tell the story of this "Christmas in a Box" project.

Christmas does sometimes come in a box—a large plastic watertight container—filled with Christmas lights, decorations, ornaments, and lots of love from people who wanted the folks in Grand Forks to have some Christmas joy.

I am tempted to sermonize about these Christmas boxes, but I suppose that any preacher or layperson can see the point: Christmas is always a gift, no matter what the packaging might be. Long ago in a dark and desperate land, to a people who were oppressed by foreign occupation, in the midst of poverty and despair, the greatest Gift came in an unusual "package"—a small, helpless baby. Who would have thought that such a gift was The Answer? So many, including the so-called "wise men," were looking for more glamorous events and more prestigious situations. Like today, many looked to celebrities and to the powerful, only to discover that God was not acting in these typical human expressions. Instead, The Gift came in an expected place, to an unexpected people, and in an unexpected form.

The year after The Flood it happened again. God surprised all of us, even those who thought that this "Christmas in a Box" idea might be helpful, as The Gift carried more meaning and hope than we ever expected.

As a friend of mine used to say, "If you can't preach about that, then you can't preach!" And if you can't see the Christmas message in that, then you won't find Christmas anywhere this year.

I pray that you will find Christmas this year:

O GOD of Surprises and Gifts,
Who blesses us in ways we never expected, help us to give and to receive the sharing that your love has reflected.

---

   *Who knew that a box full of lights and ornaments
and decorations and gifts would give so many people a sense of how your divine love can uplift?*

   *May all of us receive your gift with such joy and
surprise this season, and may all of us come to
know your surprising love is the real reason.*

Amen.

LIGHT IN THE DARKNESS

———

The people who walked in darkness
have seen a great light;
those who lived in a land of deep darkness—
on them light has shined.
(Isaiah 9:2)

———

*J*esus was born at night. All of the Christmas traditions and stories affirm this truth, and it is more than just a time of day. Jesus was born at night, he was born in the darkness, he was born to a people who were in darkness. Isaiah 9:2 is claimed by Christians as a foretelling of this truth.

Jesus was born at night, and his coming into that darkness meant light and hope for a people who were living in darkness. To a people who were repressed, conquered, poor, despairing, and almost without hope, the coming of Christ was the coming of light in the darkness.

Darkness smothers us on many levels. One thing I do not enjoy about Fargo during the winter is the length of the darkness. On the twenty-first of

———

December, the shortest day of the year, we are down to only seven and one-half hours of daylight. This means that most people go to work or school in the darkness and return in the darkness. We are so far north in latitude, and we are so far west in the Central Time Zone, that it is dark very early in the evening/late afternoon. I find that this darkness is smothering at times. Of course, I also enjoy our extremely long days in the summer, when it is possible to go for a bike ride after supper, or to take an evening walk in the twilight at 10 P.M. I guess you have to have it both ways—long days in the summer and long nights in the winter.

Darkness is also smothering in many other forms. Most all of us have spent some time in the spiritual "darkness"—in what Georgia Harkness called "the dark night of the soul." Sometimes that darkness comes in the form of grief, sometimes as depression, other times it is illness; but such dark times come into all of our lives.

The good news of Christmas is that Jesus was born at night; he was born into the darkness; and he brings the light. We tend to glamorize and sanitize his birth into a lovely creche scene; but Jesus was born at night, to a young woman who was pregnant before marriage, to a couple who were homeless on that night, to a people who were downtrodden, and to a world that was in darkness. Yet, his coming was the coming of light and hope and love into a dark world.

So, if you are in the darkness this Christmas, the good news is that Christ's coming is to bring you light. Sometimes that light has to be shared among us. Sometimes the one who most needs the light cannot see it unless it is reflected from someone nearby. Sometimes the light must be incarnated anew in our midst. However, the darkness cannot extinguish the light of Christ, and we celebrate that Jesus was born at night.

I wish you a Merry Christmas, and I pray:

O GOD
Of this holy Christmas Eve,
When the strange star shines and distant voices sing,
And in the silence a baby cries,
And shouts of praises and worship ring.

Bring us your Light in the midst of our darkness,
Shine your Light into this dark night,
Give us hope in the midst of sadness;
Show us how love can make things right.

Where some are sad in this joyous season,
Unable to feel the Christmas joy,
May your presence bring them reassurance
That you come to all in this Baby Boy.

AMEN.

A BETTER USE
OF SANDBAGS

We know that all things work together for good for those who love God, who are called according to his purpose.

(Romans 8:28)

*T*his week on the evening news I heard about a much better use of sandbags, compared to a year ago when we were involved in sandbagging against the floods of the Red River, the lake at Watertown, and elsewhere.

The East Grand Forks High School hockey team is going to the state tournament in Minnesota. At the school's pep rally, the principal declared that "E.G.F. stands for East Grand Forks, and it also stands for Everybody Got Flooded. So let's go to the state tournament and wave our new 'flags' to support our team." He then shared that over eight hundred sandbags (without the sand) would be handed out to supporters to wave and cheer for their team at the state tourney. What a great spirit to take sandbags and turn them into cheering flags! It really says something about the human spirit, doesn't it?

I have seen many people take problems and difficulties and turn them into new opportunities. I know of a mother who took the terrible loss of her

---

teenage son to cancer and used it as a motivation to help others. She has worked on a church staff welcoming newcomers, and she has led grief workshops and Bible studies to help others deal with their own grief. She took the worst possible event in her life and found a way, with God's help, to turn it into a positive.

I have seen churches do the same thing. I know of congregations that have been through fires, tornadoes, and floods who use those crisis times to become a stronger faith community. I have seen whole communities, like Grand Forks and East Grand Forks, not only survive but actually thrive after a tragedy like last year's flood.

How does that happen? How do some people respond to tragedies and problems with such grace that they turn those painful events into new avenues for growth, service, and life? Why is it that some people are overwhelmed by tragedies, never getting over the hurt and pain, while other people seem to rise to the challenge of similar tragedies?

Certainly it has to do with *attitude,* and it also has to do with *faith.* Romans 8:35-39 promises us that nothing we face in life will ever separate us from God's love in Christ Jesus: not hardship, distress, persecution, famine, nakedness, peril, or sword; neither death, life, angels, rulers, things present, things to come, powers, height, depth, or anything else in all creation. Even more, Romans 8:28 promises us that "all things work together for good for those who love God." Can we believe that? All things? It doesn't say, "All things will be good" for those who love God. Tough times and tragedies will come. The difference is our attitude and our faith in the midst of those tough times and tragedies.

So, when any circumstance comes along that the world labels a "tragedy" or a "tough time," then the question to ask is, "How is God going to make some good come out of this?" Those who seem to overcome tragedies and tough times are those who seem to have this attitude and this faith. They seem to approach such times saying simply, "God is going to be with me in this time, and God is going to help me make some good results from it."

This attitude is evident all around the Dakotas. Tough times are still tough, but God's presence helps us to endure and God's love transforms the worst of times into new opportunities to observe God at work in our midst.

At least that's what I think is happening when people take last year's sandbags and turn them into flags to cheer for their high school team. Whether their team wins or loses, they will be "winners" in life with that kind of attitude and faith.

And I pray:

O God of all the times, both troubled and easy,

Help us to recognize your presence in our lives; when the times are tough and we feel alone, give us a faith that endures and, yes, also thrives.

Thanks for the witness of those whose lives show the pain of facing tough times and tears; but whose lives also demonstrate a strong faith that survives and grows through the years.

Help us all to see your presence in the midst of such pain and heartache and despair, so that we may know the comfort and hope of seeing you work for goodness even there.

Amen.

PASTORS ARE HUMAN, TOO

But we have this treasure in clay jars, so that it may be made clear that this extraordinary power belongs to God and does not come from us. (2 Corinthians 4:7)

*P*astors are human, too. Sometimes pastors need to be reminded of that, and laity too. I recently had a series of experiences that reminded me of our human frailty as pastors.

In one twenty-four–hour period, I made pastoral calls to see a former pastor of our conference who is in prison for twenty years, a pastor who is being charged with alleged misconduct, and a pastor of our conference who is battling cancer. Some of you might be able to guess the identity of one or more of these pastors; that is not the point. I am not writing to share gossip. I am writing to tell you about our common humanity; so I will not use names, for obvious reasons.

It is quite an experience to visit someone in prison. You have to have an advance security check (although I suppose that a United Methodist bishop like me is not much of a threat to prison security); you have to show a picture ID; you are let in through a huge locked gate and escorted into a conference room. The prisoner is brought in by a guard. I have visited people in jail before, so that part wasn't new to me; but I had forgotten how all of that security feels. Most surprising was that after my visit with the ex-pastor, the guards had to search him to make sure that I had not given him anything dangerous or illegal. In fact, the only thing I had given him was my business card with my address and telephone numbers so that he can contact me. That was not considered "dangerous," so he could keep it.

He shared me with the painful reasons for his imprisonment, how much remorse he feels, and also the fact that he will struggle his whole life with the issues that resulted in his imprisonment. He also shared how much he has experienced God's grace in the midst of incarceration, how much he has grown in faith, and how grateful he is to have received over fifty Christmas cards from former parishioners and colleagues who remembered him after all of these years in jail. We prayed, he thanked me for caring, then he was searched and returned to his cell. I must admit that the cold, fresh air of freedom outside that prison felt good.

My second call was to see a pastor who is being accused of misconduct. He is embarrassed, ashamed, confused, and very concerned not to damage the church. He said, "So many people have put me on a pedestal; now what are they going to think?" He offered to give me his ordination credentials on the spot. (I told him, "Not now. We will have to see how this whole process concludes.") I told him that I was disappointed, but I also tried to reassure him that the positive aspects of his ministry are not erased by this one episode. We prayed together about his uncertain future and his possible loss of credentials.

My third call in that twenty-four–hour period was to see a pastor of our conference who is battling cancer. I had hoped to encourage him, but instead I discovered that he was able to minister to me. He shared several new books that have helped him; he told me what a wonderful thing it is to learn that "we are not indispensable" as pastors; and he bragged about all the things the laity of his churches are now doing to help with the ministry while he is ill. He was realistic about his cancer, but he was also optimistic about how God is working through his situation. Before I could offer a prayer, he prayed for me—for my health, my traveling safety, and my ministry as his bishop. Then he quickly ushered me out, because someone was coming by to see him who needed help. I left feeling truly amazed by his faithful witness in the midst of such illness.

I share these three visits with you to remind all of us (including me) how human we are. No pastor ever intends to commit a crime or misconduct that will ruin a ministry and damage a church's trust. No pastor expects to become too ill to perform ministry. But it happens. In our humanity, we are all frail, filled with possibilities for failure, and yet recipients of God's grace. Someone once said that we are all "equally unworthy" of the grace of God. I believe that, and I believe that we must be "real" about our humanity.

In my experience, the pastors most likely to get into trouble are those who do not believe that they are human. In their naiveté, they think, "It couldn't happen to me"—until they find themselves making such mistakes or suffering from such tragedies. Other pastors recognize their humanity, take care to avoid compromising situations, and draw their boundaries of behavior very carefully.

In my experience, the pastors who cannot handle sickness or failure or tragedies are those who believe that they are "above" such things, or who believe that God will protect them from such problems. When those things come along, they are unprepared to deal with them. Other pastors recognize their humanity, see life as a gift, and look for God's presence even in the midst of illness and problems.

It all seems to depend upon recognizing our humanity, knowing that we are human and accepting it. Maybe it also depends upon truly believing that God is God—and not me (or us). Above all, it depends upon being willing to accept our humanity *and* to accept God's grace as a gift that none of us deserves.

All of us are human, and pastors are human, too. I pray:

O LORD,
You have created us to be human,
And none can be more than that, it seems;
Frailty, failure, and faults are always with us,
In spite of our efforts, or even our dreams.

Your love, O Lord, is all that sustains us,
Freeing us, filling us, giving us grace
To know being human is just who we are,
It is part of running in the human race.

Pastors are human, too, and yet we forget
To allow ourselves to be human like others;
Sometimes we try to be something we're not,
Sometimes we use "pastor" as our cover.

Help us, O Lord, to accept each other
And help us to accept ourselves, too.
Give us your grace to sustain, and then help us
To live as you are calling us to.

AMEN.

SAP
ON THE FAMILY TREE

There is no longer Jew or Greek, there is no longer slave or free, there is no longer male and female; for all of you are one in Christ Jesus. (Galatians 3:28)

I have been receiving communications from a man named Coyner Smith. He first contacted me after I was elected a United Methodist bishop and assigned to the Dakotas. He is from Nebraska, and he wondered if we might be related. Through letters and telephone calls we have been able to determine that we have the same great-great-grandmother, Elizabeth Rhea Coyner. Mr. Smith is from the part of the Smith family that intermarried with the Rhea family that intermarried with the Coyner family; hence his name (which was also his grandfather's name).

Mr. Coyner Smith recently sent me a copy of the last will and testament of my great-great-great-grandfather, whose name was Michael Coiner (the Coyner family comes from the original Michael Keinadt of Germany, and our family branches spell the name as Koiner, Koyner, Coiner, Coyner, and other variations). Anyway, I was rather excited to have a copy of the will of my ancestor, Michael Coiner, of Virginia, written in 1798.

When I read the document carefully, I discovered that one of the "possessions" that my ancestor left in his will was a slave woman named Sall. What a shock! I guess I knew intellectually that some of my ancestors in Virginia might have been slave-owners, but to see it in print was quite disturbing. My family, my ancestors, and someone with whom I share the name Michael Coiner, was a slave-owner! He mentions the woman named Sall so indifferently— just one of his pieces of property. On an attached document she is listed with a value of $200, just as one of his horses is listed with a value of $115.

It is a terrible thing to realize that my family was involved in slave-owning and that they considered an African American woman named Sall as a piece of property.

Racism is a sin that is still with us. Racism is the largest social problem that we face in America, and all of us have inherited the terrible results of the evil system of slavery that dominated this country. Racism allowed our ancestors to treat African Americans as slaves. Here in the Dakotas racism allowed our ancestors to exterminate the Native American peoples to make room for white "progress." And this racism still plagues all the various people groups in our country.

Racism is damaging to white people, too. Racism has led us to depersonalize others, to see them as different, to disregard our common humanity. Racism has caused us to assume that our privileges and positions are somehow earned, even when they have come on the backs of other people. Racism has kept us from accepting fully the gospel as good news for all. Racism has prevented us from having the appropriate humility of heart and soul that prepares us to receive God's grace. Racism has caused us to violate the most basic commandment of Jesus, that we love one another as he loves us. And yet racism is here, in every family, in every part of our society, in every aspect of our culture.   It is dangerous to look too closely at one's family tree, isn't it? I wonder why Michael Coiner so easily accepted slavery as a part of life in Virginia in the 1700's. I wonder whatever became of Sall, what happened to her children and grandchildren, and whether any of her descendants have had the opportunity to study their family tree. I wonder if we will ever fulfill the vision that "there is no longer slave or free." And I wonder if my great-great-great-grandchildren will be free of racism.

God forgive us all, and may God help us to overcome this plague of racism.

I pray:

O GOD,
You made us all so much alike,
No matter color or race, we are like each other;
Why can't we live in harmony with all,
And come to know each person as a sister or a brother?

Color of skin or eyes or hair doesn't matter,
And yet we quickly judge, hate, and condemn;
Why can't we see the child of God in each other
As we follow Jesus and learn to love like him?

Our families are full of mistakes and errors,
And all of us are victims of a less-than-perfect past;
Help us to end the sins of racism and hatred
And bring us a better and brighter tomorrow at last.
                                                    AMEN.

CONNECTED BY THE INNER NET

For just as the body is one and has many members, and all the members of the body, though many, are one body, so it is with Christ. *(1 Corinthians 12:12)*

I have recently received two surprise e-mail messages that reminded me of how connected we really are. One message came from Bob Douglass, a friend from high school from whom I had not heard in over thirty years. Bob and I were in the same home church, played together on the church basketball team, lived in the same neighborhood, and were good friends. But with the march of time, we had lost track of each other. His mother (who still lives back in Indiana) knew that I had been elected a bishop, so Bob looked for my e-mail address on the Internet under "bishop" and "coyner," and he found me (which is one reason why I use that simple e-mail address). Receiving an e-mail message from him last week was quite a surprise, and now we are using e-mail to get reacquainted across the years and the miles.

The second message was even more surprising. It was from Ana Christina, a young woman whom I met on a mission trip to Brazil in 1993. Our district sent mission work teams to help her church in Campina Grande build their new church sanctuary building. Ana is a musician, speaks very good English, and is now on the Internet. So she found my address through a United Methodist pastor in Indiana, and she has been communicating with me (from Brazil) by e-mail. It has been wonderful to hear from her about the progress of their Methodist mission church in Brazil, which is now self-sufficient and supporting three other Methodist pastors doing evangelism and outreach ministry. Especially it has been interesting to have Ana respond to my "Life in the Dakotas" messages from her perspective as a Brazilian.

Those two examples remind me of how connected we are. It is a small world, and we are not very far removed from one another. Experts say we are only seven relationships away from anyone else anywhere in the world, which means that you know somebody, who knows somebody, who knows somebody, who knows somebody, who knows somebody, who knows somebody, who knows any other person in the world. I am not sure how the experts can ever prove that, but it seems to be true!

So I sit in my office in Fargo, North Dakota, and I am connected with Bob in Seattle and with Ana Christina in Brazil. I am also connected with hundreds of other persons by e-mail, many of whom forward my "Life in the Dakotas" reflections on to other friends and relatives. We are all "connected," and the world seems smaller and closer.

And yet . . . we are already connected in ways that are even more intimate. A few years ago I heard a wonderful devotion about the "Inner Net" of our connection by prayer, and the leader reminded us that this "Inner Net" has been available to us long before the "Internet" became available and popular. By our thoughts and prayers we are connected in ways that are far more amazing than anything computers and e-mail can provide. By prayer, I am connected to all of the three hundred churches of the Dakotas Conference. By prayer, I can "travel" anywhere around the world and provide caring and support for any other person. By prayer, I can be "present" with any other person in ways that are beyond our typical physical existence. By prayer, God's Spirit links our human spirits with one another and with God's own Spirit. This "Inner Net" connects us in ways that are so much more profound than any denominational structures or any communication technology.

It is good to be connected with you by e-mail, and it is even better when we are connected by the Inner Net that God has provided for us.

And so I pray:

O LORD,
Keep us close to you, through your Spirit,
And keep us connected to each other, too.
Remind us that we all belong to each other,
Remind us of our connection to you.

By prayer we can be anywhere or anytime
Present with those we love and for whom we care;
No matter what distance or years or time and space,
By prayer we can instantaneously be there.

And so you have designed us for intimate fellowship
With each other and also with you;
No one has to feel alone, left out, or forgotten
When life is viewed from your view.

AMEN.

THANKS EL NIÑO

[Jesus] said to them, "Take care! Be on your guard against all kinds of greed; for one's life does not consist in the abundance of possessions."   (Luke 12:15)

I saw the sign just outside of Pierre, South Dakota. It reads simply, "Thanks El Niño." The sign reflects the way most of us in the Dakotas are feeling this year—grateful for a mild winter, relieved that the storms and blizzards of last year have stayed away (so far) this year, and hopeful that we will avoid the terrible floods and damaging losses of last year. In fact, the temperature has been in the upper-30's and rain is falling here in Fargo during this mid-February time—such a contrast to last year! Oh yes, we still have a little snow on the ground, but our streets are dry and our total snow-fall this season is only up to about twenty-five inches; whereas at this time last year we had over eighty inches of snow on the ground, temperatures were below zero for days, and we were besieged again and again by winds and blizzards.

People are even beginning to joke a little about our weather (something we did not do last year). In Mitchell, South Dakota, last week where the snow was limited to small, leftover piles around the edges of parking lots, someone from the Black Hills area said to me, "What is that white stuff on the ground?" Those folks from the Black Hills are always bragging about their wonderful weather. They even call their area the Banana Belt of the Dakotas. I responded by saying, "I was wondering what that brown stuff is on the ground." But truthfully, it was good to see some of the brown grass this year in February. What a difference from last year when we didn't see anything but snow from the middle of November until very early in April.

"Thanks El Niño"—indeed!

However, the same El Niño that has brought us a milder winter has clobbered the east coast and the west coast of this country with terrible storms, ice, rain, and tides. It is hard to feel very good about our milder winter when we can also watch on TV the news about the bad weather elsewhere. I suppose that is how others felt last year when they watched the news and saw our terrible weather here in the Dakotas.

It really is a problem, isn't it? We can't just be thankful to God for our good fortune. It is really too simplistic to pray, "Thank God for blessing us this year" without some awareness that our good weather is related to the bad weather that others are experiencing. I believe that one of the most shallow of all prayers is the prayer that thanks God for one's own good life while ignoring the impact that good life has upon others. Too often we are only grateful for our privileges and status, while being unconcerned that the result of our blessings may be misery for others.

That is why I don't pray for stoplights to change to green for me. I have actually heard well-meaning Christians say that they pray for green lights, for parking places at the mall, and for other trivial concerns. They proclaim, "God takes care of my needs!" Is that true? Is that really the basis of their faith? Does God really change a traffic light to green for them without regard to what changing to red does to the other drivers? That's not how I understand God's blessings.

Let me share an example. Every year the US Department of Agriculture releases a study about the supply of food for the world, and nearly every year the report states that enough food is being produced in our world to feed the entire population of the world. So what is the problem? Why are some people (like us in the USA) so overfed, while others are starving? The problem is politics, lack of concern, a poor distribution system, and gluttony by some while others starve.

God provides the food (including the human ability to create the technology to produce the harvest) for all of God's children. Shall some of us pray gratefully that we are fed, while ignoring the fact that others are hungry? Shall some of us think only of our blessings, without also caring that God's blessings are not being evenly distributed? Is it enough just to be thankful that I can eat? Am I not also to be concerned about those who don't eat?

These prayers of thanksgiving for our blessings that we offer so quickly—these prayers are dangerously close to hypocrisy, aren't they? It is so tempting just to be grateful for our good fortune, while forgetting the needs and hurts of others.

Jesus put it this way, " 'Take care! Be on your guard against all kinds of greed; for one's life does not consist in the abundance of possessions.' . . . 'You fool! This very night your life is being demanded of you. And the things you have prepared, whose will they be?' So it is with those who store up treasures for themselves but are not rich toward God" (Luke 12:15, 20-21).

So, thanks for El Niño; but let's not be greedy about our mild winter and unaware of the tragic results of El Niño for others. Maybe this is the year that we in the Dakotas are called to send offerings and work teams to other parts of the country (and the world). Maybe our blessings are given to us in order for us to share with others.

And I pray:

O Lord,

It is easy to be thankful for all the blessings that come our way without giving much thought to their impact upon others. Help us to remember to look at our good fortune and to pray for the needs of all the rest of our sisters and brothers.

El Niño has been such a blessing to us in the Dakotas, yet it has caused rain and destruction elsewhere. So we thank you, Lord, for the relief that we feel in our area, but we ask you to comfort those in need everywhere.

Give us the courage to stand during the tough times, to know your presence and your strength are so near; but help us to remember to thank you just as much when we are enjoying a much easier year.

Amen.

CLONING NAOMI

We have gifts that differ according to the grace given to us: prophecy, in proportion to faith; ministry, in ministering; the teacher, in teaching; the exhorter, in exhortation; the giver, in generosity; the leader, in diligence; the compassionate, in cheerfulness. (Romans 12:6-8)

No one is indispensable, but some of us are more necessary than others. That's why I might be willing to waive our denominational opposition to "cloning" just long enough to clone Naomi. Let me tell you about Naomi.

Naomi Bartle has been the bishop's secretary here in the Dakotas Area Office since the office moved from Aberdeen, South Dakota, to Fargo, North Dakota, in 1980. She opened the office, and she has been here through three bishops (so far) and two changes of location of the office here in Fargo. She is experienced; thorough; capable; friendly; caring; and committed deeply to God, the church, and the bishop (and she has those in the right order). When I arrived here in 1996, still very "green" and new to this bishop thing, Naomi was a wonderful help to me. She knows everyone in the conference and she knows the history behind most of our issues.

Naomi is excellent at keeping confidentiality, and she understands that working in a bishop's office is not always fun—it includes hearing some sad stories and dealing with some tough issues. Some days she reminds me of "Radar" in the old *M*A*S*H* television series, because she brings me files and information before I have a chance to ask for them (or even know that I need to ask for them). In a word, Naomi is more indispensable than most of us. In fact, one of the jokes around here is, "Don't let anything happen to Naomi. We can always go to the Jurisdictional Conference and get another bishop, but we don't know where we could find another Naomi."

Let me give you an example. Recently Naomi went on a well-deserved vacation. The first day I was in the office during her absence, the following things went wrong: the copier machine stopped working its automatic feeder, and I had to place originals by hand; the coffee machine stopped working, and even when I found the reset button it still would not stay on for more than two minutes; the mail wasn't delivered (OK, it was President's Day, but still I wasn't used to the mail not being delivered, opened, and sorted for me); and the florescent lights in my office started blinking and finally went out! Luckily I was leaving town on Tuesday for the rest of the week, so I don't know what else might have stopped working if I had stayed around! I suspect that our office equipment just didn't know how to function with Naomi out of the office—or else the equipment thought that if Naomi was on vacation, then it should be, too.

There is a "Naomi" in most every organization and in most every church. It may be a church secretary, an organist, a janitor, a women's group president, a lay leader, or a long-time "saint" who is now homebound. These indispensable people are the backbone of every institution. They love their work, they love their opportunity to serve, and they love the people who come and go. They are "servant leaders" in the best sense of that term.

Unfortunately, these persons are often overlooked or taken for granted. My grandmother counted the offering each Sunday for over thirty-five years in her little Methodist church in Colfax, Indiana. Sure it was convenient for her to do that job: she lived just across the street from the church, and her husband (my grandfather) was the manager of the little branch bank there in town. Still, I wonder how many times in all of those years anyone thanked her for doing that job. I wonder about the volunteer organists and pianists in our churches—how many times do they receive a word of appreciation? And how about those men (and women) who always mow the lawn, shovel the snow, or do one of the many other odd jobs that are necessary around the church. Do we stop and say "Thanks" to them? Or how about the perpetual youth counselors, some of whom are grandparents now; do we thank them for loving our youth and putting up with the things that youth always do?

When Naomi gets back from vacation, I am going to thank her for all that she does. And then I am going to ask her how to fix the copier, the coffee machine, and the florescent lights in my office.

Just one more thing, during these infrequent times when Naomi is gone from the office, please don't sound so disappointed when you call and get me on the phone instead of Naomi. Several people have already called, heard my voice, and said, "Oh, sorry Bishop, I needed to talk to Naomi." Please, when you call and get me instead of Naomi, just humor me a little, and pretend that you think I might know the answer to your question. I can always take a message and ask Naomi later!

And I pray:

O LORD,
Thank you for Naomi and for all the others
Who minister to us and help us to succeed;
Somehow they know just the word to say and
What to do and what we really need.

"Servant leadership" is a catchy phrase today
And lots of books talk about this panacea;
But many folks in our lives have already been
Living examples of this ancient idea.

Thank you, Lord, for those who help and serve,
For those who give themselves in love;
For they remind us of the One who served
And who now leads us from above.

                                                            AMEN.

SHAVED HEADS

For this reason I remind you to rekindle the gift of God that is within you through the laying on of my hands; for God did not give us a spirit of cowardice, but rather a spirit of power and of love and of self-discipline.

(2 Timothy 1:6-7)

*H*ave you noticed all of the shaved heads in the NBA playoffs? Many of the professional basketball players have shaved their heads as a sign of commitment to excel during the playoffs. This has led to the observation that some heads look better shaved than others. Michael Jordan of the Chicago Bulls, for example, looks tough, athletic, and rather handsome with his shaved head. I have never considered shaving my own head, but I suspect that with a shaved head and a white pulpit robe I would look a little too much like the Pillsbury Doughboy®. Shaved heads are not for everyone.

I received an e-mail from one of our Dakotas Conference pastors informing me that he has shaved his head in solidarity with one of his parishioners who is battling cancer. Scott Mendez-Andrews says that he was inspired by a story he read a few years ago about a fourth-grade boy who lost his hair during chemotherapy. To show their support, all of his classmates shaved their heads too. Scott says that having his head shaved reminds him to pray for his parishioner, and it also reminds others to pray for her.

Scott reports: "Since I shaved my head last Tuesday, some amazing things have happened. All three of my churches have rallied around [my parishioner]. One of the churches has organized a pancake supper to help offset some of her medical expenses. People on the street have started to say to me, 'I prayed for [her] today.' I had no idea that such a simple thing could have such an impact. As a matter of fact, to rub my head will now cost you $100—with the money going to help pay for medical expenses."

I honor and respect the kind of commitment that causes a person to shave his or her head, especially for ministry. In a few weeks when Scott is ordained an elder in the Dakotas Conference, it will be an honor for me to lay hands on his shaved head.

All of this leads me to wonder, for whom or for what do I have enough passion to shave my head (either literally or figuratively)? How about you? For what are you passionate? Are you passionate about reaching the unchurched for Christ? Are you passionate about youth ministry, or children's ministry, or older adult ministry? Are you passionate about ministering to the poor and to "the least of these"? Are you passionate about having our church be an inclusive church where all of God's children are welcome? Are you passionate about anything?

Much of what we do in the life of our churches and our ministry is not worthy of much passion. Much of ministry and much of life can be rather mundane. That's OK. Sometimes we do ministry out of obedience, whether we feel very passionate that day or not. The question is, do we have a passion that continues to empower our ministry?

In the vision statement that has been adopted by our Dakotas Conference, we talk about "participating in God's harvest" as the focus of our ministry. The vision statement says that the motivation for participating in God's harvest is "a passion for God and a passion for people." That must be true for any vision statement to have power in our churches and in our ministry. Only a passion for ministry can lead us to look beyond our own church doors, beyond our comfort zone, and beyond our usual way of doing things. It requires passion to care enough to participate in God's harvest. Our vision statement will not mean much unless it taps into a passion that can empower our ministry as a conference.

So, I ask you (and myself) again: Where is your passion? Are you ready to "shave your head"?

And I pray:

O Lord,

Give us passion for ministry, not just more of the same. Don't let us go through the motions, but lead us forth in your name.

Our ministry requires more than obedience, so it seems, and we need to aspire, to reach out, and to dream some new dreams.

So, give us your passion and your energy and your drive, fill us with vision to keep our ministry, our churches, and ourselves alive.

Amen.

NOTICING ONE ANOTHER

Beloved, let us love one another, because love is from God; everyone who loves is born of God and knows God. Whoever does not love does not know God, for God is love. God's love was revealed among us in this way: God sent his only Son into the world so that we might live through him. In this is love, not that we loved God but that he loved us and sent his Son to be the atoning sacrifice for our sins.   *(1 John 4:7-10)*

Among the good and wonderful traits of the people here in the Dakotas is another one that goes unmentioned: people notice each other. I have walked the streets of many larger cities in the US where almost no one makes eye contact with anyone, and very few people say "Hello" to passing strangers. Here in the Dakotas, it is not at all unusual for people to take notice of one another and to say "Hello" or some other greeting. It doesn't happen everywhere, but it happens here more than I have experienced elsewhere.

Of course, there are exceptions. People are people, "folks are folks" here, too, and some people don't notice others whom they would like to avoid.

The most typical group of overlooked people is our Native American population. Another ethnic group that may be missed is our Hispanic population, which is small but growing. It is easier to say "Hello" to people who look like us, isn't it?

One of our young pastors who lives and serves in a community that is literally in the midst of a reservation shared this song with me and gave me permission to share it with you:

"The One You Don't See," by Rev. DeAnn Eidem

You passed me by the other day
You didn't even look my way
Blinded by this wall we've made
Formed of anger, fear and hate.
But let us sing a song of praise
And ask the Lord to bless our way
And if our paths should cross again
Look through me
It's easy.

Stopped by my church to sit awhile
So many memories make me smile
Wrapped up in these arms of love
Countless blessings from above
This grace is made for big and small
And difference matters not at all.
So isn't it strange
We all look the same.

But thus says the Lord your God
Before you were born I knew the feel of your tiny
    hand
And I held you in my heart.
You and your sister
You and your brother
The one you don't see.

O Lord, You know each part of me
I need Your strength to set me free
Cast away these chains that bind
And clear the blindness from my eyes.
Oh, help me learn to be like You
To show Your love as You would do.
Lord, let Your love be born again
In my heart.
In my heart.

I can't add much to her beautiful words, and I hope to hear her sing them sometime. Perhaps she is a modern-day echo of the words of 1 John 4:7-12, which Eugene Peterson has translated in *The Message* to say: "My beloved friends, let us continue to love each other since love comes from God. Everyone who loves is born of God and experiences a relationship with God. The person who refuses to love doesn't know the first thing about God, because God is love—so you can't know him if you don't love. . . . My dear, dear friends, if God loved us like this, we certainly ought to love each other. No one has seen God, ever. But if we love one another, God dwells deeply within us, and his love becomes complete in us—perfect love!"[1]

DeAnn's song reminds us that loving one another begins with noticing one another, not walking by, avoiding eye contact, and pretending that the "stranger" doesn't even exist.

So, keep on noticing one another, even when the "other" is someone who is quite different. Keep on saying "Hello" and smiling and offering words of acknowledgment to one another. Because love is

---

[1] From *The Message: The New Testament in Contemporary Language*; by Eugene H. Peterson; NavPress; 1993; page 506.

from God, and loving our neighbor starts with noticing that our neighbor even exists.

And so I pray:

O Lord,
Help us to notice each other,
Help us to really see,
That everyone is so much alike,
Everyone is so much like me.

Our differences are easy to notice,
Our color, our hair, our ethnicities;
It is too easy to see these differences
And to miss our similarities.

Help us to notice and see each other,
To treat each one as a sister and brother;
Help us to see the family resemblance
And to notice God's Spirit in each other.

Amen.

TOO MUCH "VITAMIN I" IS BAD FOR OUR HEALTH

I therefore, the prisoner in the Lord, beg you to lead a life worthy of the calling to which you have been called, with all humility and gentleness, with patience, bearing with one another in love, making every effort to maintain the unity of the Spirit in the bond of peace. (Ephesians 4:1-3)

The Dakotas Annual Conference meets next week, and most of the other annual conferences of United Methodism will also be meeting in the next few weeks. These annual conference sessions are a wonderful combination of family reunion, political convention, revival, business meeting, education, and social gathering. I always enjoy attending annual conference, and back in North Indiana that was one of the places where I experienced "family" and "church." This is especially true since all United Methodist clergy are members of conferences, not of local churches. We love and serve our local churches, but our annual conference is, for us, our "local church" where we meet and fellowship with colleagues.

Since being elected a bishop and having to preside at annual conference, I miss some of the informal moments of conference; but I still enjoy the session each year. (Let me translate that: before I was a bishop, I could spend significant time talking with people over coffee or ice cream; but now I have to sit up front and preside for the whole session.) There is nothing quite like a United Methodist annual conference session, and I look forward to ours next week.

One part of annual conference is especially significant: we gather to make decisions as a group, as a community of faith, as a people of God. Belonging to a United Methodist church means that we are in covenant with one another to act together. We are not Lone Rangers simply doing our own thing in ministry; we are members of a group/family/covenant where we decide and act together. For that to happen, all of us give up a little of our individual freedom in order to be a part of a greater cause. For that to happen, we need to be careful not to overdose on "Vitamin I."

My mail recently has been filled with the letter "I," from different sorts of people all over the country on various issues. But the one constant theme from each writer has been to express, "I believe . . ." or "I think . . ." or "The Bible tells me. . . ." While everyone's individual opinion is important, that is not how we United Methodists function. We make decisions together, we "conference" with one another, we look for God's guidance through the total group, and we know—as one person told me recently— "None of us is as smart as all of us."

It really is a basic theological and epistemological issue: what do we know about God and how do we know what we know? For us as United Methodists, the answer is, "We know about God together as a faith community." This is more than just democracy or Robert's Rules of Order. We believe that God works through the body of Christ in the world today, and we know that God's wisdom and discernment are discovered when we gather as God's people. Any one of us may be misled, may misinterpret Scripture, may make decisions that are prejudiced by our own limited experiences and understanding. Together, as the whole people of God, we have a chance to test our wisdom and our discernment against that of others; and we can receive a greater guidance from the whole body. To know and believe and act together is a basic part of what it means to be a United Methodist.

Is our United Methodist approach to life countercultural today? It certainly is! We live in a country and in a time when individualism is a god that is worshiped and adored. Just watch some of the commercials on TV or listen to some of the conversations at the coffee shop or the grain elevator. The whole focus of our culture is upon "I"—What's in it for me? What is my preference? How do I get what I want?

We applaud individual effort, we celebrate the individual who buys the winning lottery ticket without any regard for the millions of other people who wasted their money buying losing tickets, and we even seem to regard as "heroes" those who cheat to get ahead of others. This individualism carries over into religion. So much of my mail has been from individuals who claim to have the right answer, the only interpretation of Scripture, and the best sense of God's will for our world or for our church. One person even wrote to me, "I don't care about church doctrine and tradition, I can read the Bible for myself."

Yes, our United Methodist style of seeking God's

wisdom as a group is countercultural. Next week when we gather as a Dakotas Conference for our annual conference session, we will actually surrender some of our individual "rights" in order to seek God's wisdom through the discussion, debate, discernment, and voting of the total group. It is not an easy way to make decisions, and certainly it is not the fastest way to make decisions (maybe that's why some have written to me from around the country demanding that the bishops "take charge" and "fix" our church), but it is the United Methodist way. And I believe it is the best way.

And so I pray:

———————

O LORD,
Forgive me whenever I start to think
That I understand what the church is meant to be.
Keep me from being too local and too limited,
Remind me that "church" is much more than I can
*   see.*

Whenever I think that my own little issues
Are the only important things that face us today,
Remind me that your church is so much larger
Than the limited role I am called to play.

Thank you for the witness of those from other lands
And for the churches and ministries that they do.
Remind me that we are all part of your family
Doing the various ministries that you call us to do.
*   AMEN.*

———————

GOOD-BYE, BANDIT

T hen God said to Noah and to his sons with him, "As for me, I am establishing my covenant with you and your descendants after you, and with every living creature that is with you, the birds, the domestic animals, and every animal of the earth with you, as many as came out of the ark." (Genesis 9:8-10)

*J*une 26 was a very sad day in the Coyner household. That was the day that our old dog Bandit died, after being a part of our family for nearly fourteen years.

In October of 1984, a little stray dog (mixed breed) showed up in our parsonage yard in South Bend, Indiana, with a hurt leg after having been dumped by someone who didn't want him. After my wife Marsha and our two children helped this little dog recover, he made himself at home. All of this occurred while I was out of town, and my only clue was when I called home and our son Steve (who was six at the time) yelled into the phone, "We have a surprise, but I can't tell you about it!" So, I wasn't too surprised to come home and find that we had a new member of the family.

As we searched for a name for this little dog, we noticed that his coloring included a kind of mask across his eyes. So we named him Bandit—because he had stolen into our home and into our hearts. He was about a year old at the time, and we never would have guessed that he would be with us for so many years.

At first Bandit wasn't too sure about me or any other men. He was especially frightened by my shoes, and so we assume he might have been kicked and abused by some man previously. From the very first day, he loved and played with our kids, and he was also a "shadow" who followed Marsha around everywhere she went. This behavior continued throughout the years, even in recent months when moving and walking were more difficult for him.

I guess the amazing thing about Bandit was his ability to adapt. He moved right into our home and our lives in South Bend, then followed us as we moved to Fort Wayne, to West Lafayette, to a different house in West Lafayette, and then on to Fargo, North Dakota. Everywhere we moved, he moved right along—somehow able to adapt and to be at home in any new situation. He was always the first to meet the new neighbors (in mostly positive circumstances), and he seemed to enjoy discovering his new surroundings in every community. He never liked riding in the car or van, but when we moved to new places he seemed to understand that those long trips were necessary to follow us to a new home.

Bandit also provided all of us (and most everyone he met) with unconditional love. I read somewhere that the best any of us can hope for is to be the wonderful person that our dog thinks we are.

As Marsha put it when we moved to Fargo, "I don't know if I could make this move without our little buddy." Bandit had a way of making the best out of every situation, enjoying life, and loving people.

One of the people who really took to Bandit in Fargo was Jerry Wickre. Jerry was the district superintendent in the Fargo area, and he and his wife Linda enjoyed Bandit enough that they offered to take care of him when we were out of town at meetings like the Council of Bishops. Linda referred to Bandit as "our furry friend." After Jerry died suddenly in the fall of 1996, Linda still wanted to take care of Bandit. Somehow I think that Bandit helped her with the grief and loss she felt after Jerry's death. Nearly two years afterward, Linda and her new husband stopped by Fargo to see us—and it seemed Bandit was the one she was the most pleased to see. Bandit was getting more feeble by then, but he still remembered Linda and seemed to approve of her husband Warren.

Dogs don't live forever, and Bandit slowly weakened this spring. He no longer led us on our evening walks, he dragged along behind. A trip to the vet confirmed that Bandit's kidneys were no longer functioning, and the vet predicted that Bandit would not live more than one or two more days. Marsha called me with that sad news because I was out of town (where else?) and she warned me that Bandit would not live until I got home.

Once again, Bandit seemed to know that his presence was important, and he rallied for a few more days of life. He even showed occasional spurts of his old lively style, after which he tired quickly. He did live until I got home, and so I was glad for the chance to say good-bye to our old friend.

He stole into our lives nearly fourteen years ago, and he stole out again just as quickly. In between he taught us a lot about life, about giving love, about adapting to new circumstances, and about making a "home" wherever our family moved.

Thank you, Bandit. And good-bye.

And so I pray:

O LORD,
Thank you for all creatures, both great and small,
Thank you for the gift of their lives to each of us;
Thanks for the way these pets become a part of our
*   hearts,*
Moving right in to love and to be with us.

How sad it would be to never know the joy of these
*   furry friends,*
How empty our homes and lives would be;
So thanks for those with fours legs and fur and tails
Who seem to love life and know how to just be.

In all of our sophistication, with all of our knowl-
*   edge,*
And with all of our electronic toys,
Thanks for the reminder that pets seem to bring,
That life is best filled with simple joys.
                                          AMEN.

HORSING AROUND THE BADLANDS

---

*P*raise the LORD!

Praise God in his sanctuary;

praise him in his mighty firmament! . . .

Let everything that breathes praise the LORD!

Praise the LORD!

(Psalm 150:1, 6)

---

*L*ast weekend was one of those perfect, memorable times in the Dakotas. Our son Steve was home for the end of summer before going back to college in the fall, and so Marsha and I took him to Medora, North Dakota, to visit the Theodore Roosevelt National Park there in the Badlands of North Dakotas.

The Badlands in North Dakota (and the similar Badlands in South Dakota) are among the most beautiful places that I have ever visited. The Badlands rival the Grand Canyon, although on a smaller scale. The formations of color, water, sand, and landscape are breathtaking, and a drive through the Badlands is filled with one "photo opportunity" after another.

We stayed overnight in Medora, a small Western town, and enjoyed eating dinner at the Iron Horse Saloon and breakfast at the Cowboy Cafe. We stayed in the Badlands Motel, and we were awakened every few hours by the trains passing through. Best of all, we went horseback riding around the Badlands on a beautiful Sunday evening. The sky was a perfect blue, the humidity was low, and a nice breeze was blowing. This was the first time on horseback for me and for Steve, but we did well. Our horses had interesting names. Marsha rode on Romeo, a blue-eyed horse who "prefers to have beautiful women as his riders." Steve rode on Rascal, a name that fits Steve's mischievous personality, and I rode on Ben, who was described as a horse "who only likes to eat and sleep." I am not sure how they selected the horses for us, but I really don't want to know. We rode across the Little Missouri River; we saw deer, buffalo, and hundreds of prairie dogs; and we thoroughly enjoyed the scenery.

After returning to Fargo, we enjoyed time riding bikes (a more familiar mode of transportation for me) in the beauty of summer evenings here in North Dakota. The temperature was mid-80's, the humidity was 38 percent, and a perfectly blue sky was offset by the brilliant yellow sunflowers that are growing in the field behind our housing addition. Summer evenings in Fargo can have that kind of "perfect" quality, with our long days providing opportunity for bike rides as late as 9:30 or 10:00 P.M.

All of which reminds me of what someone told me when we moved here: "Winters can be hell in the Dakotas, but it is worth it to enjoy the summers here." We have certainly found that to be true. In winter you sometimes have to endure huge amounts of snow, cold, and wind; but then summer comes with warm temperatures, clear skies, gentle breezes, and beautiful scenery. Having endured a Dakotas winter makes a Dakotas summer even more perfect.

I suppose much of life is like that—you have to endure the tough times in order to really enjoy the good times. A family is always more appreciated when you have had to live through times of conflict, separation, or growing pains. A marriage means more after you have experienced aloneness or grief. Love means more in the context of struggle and change. Faith means more when it helps us to overcome pain and fear. Life has more meaning after we have looked directly into the face of illness and death.

I feel sorry for those who live in perfect weather year-round. I am sure it must be nice to live in Hawaii, for example; but don't all of those perfect days get to be routine? Don't people take that for granted?

I feel sorry for those who have never suffered or been hurt in life. They have missed the opportunity to grow through tough times and to discover their true friends and their true faith.

I often tell parents that I hope their children will disappoint them sometime, because otherwise you never get a chance to demonstrate to your children that you love them in spite of their mistakes.

I have even told married couples that they should look forward to tough times in their marriage, because that will be the opportunity to grow closer together—and the "making up" time can be fun, too!

God has blessed us here in the Dakotas (and most

everywhere else, too) with some terrible weather that helps the good weather and the good moments seem even more enjoyable. Last weekend was one of those times—time to spend with our young-adult son who is growing up fast and spending less and less time in the family nest, time to enjoy the beauty of God's world, time to see and to share some incredible landscapes, and time to simply enjoy life.

And so I pray:

O LORD,

Thank you for the tough times, for the storms and the blizzards and the snows; and thank you Lord for the summers, when the sun shines and a softer wind blows. Tough times make the good times even better, more aware of your goodness and love. So thank you, Lord, for providing this variety of life from above.

Thank you, Lord, for tough times in our relationships, times filled with growing pains. Those times challenge us to grow and to mature, for without pain there is no gain. Thank you, Lord, for the problems that stretch us and make us learn new ways. Help us to grow from these challenges and learn to follow your path always.

Thank you that each winter is followed by summer, with spring bringing hope anew. Thanks that the winters don't last forever, and even in Fargo there is time to renew. Fill our lives with your goodness, and give us your love and care, so that the tough times may be times of learning to trust you anytime, anywhere.

AMEN.

WHAT AM I SELLING?

Blessed be the God and Father of our Lord Jesus Christ! By his great mercy he has given us a new birth into a living hope through the resurrection of Jesus Christ from the dead. (1 Peter 1:3)

Now that I have been the bishop of the Dakotas Conference of The United Methodist Church for nearly two years, please allow me to do a little reflecting on my role as bishop. The following images have been offered to me by various people in the Dakotas. While I would not say that I am fulfilling any of these images completely, they do provide me with some directions and goals for my ministry as a bishop.

1. Several people have told me that I am a "pastors' bishop" and that I seem to spend much of my time trying to encourage the pastors of our conference, providing leadership training events for those pastors, and being a "pastor to the pastors." I do think of myself primarily as a pastor, so I hope that I can be a "pastors' bishop" without ignoring our laity.

2. Some laypersons have told me that I seem to be able to understand the issues facing local

---

churches of various sizes. If this is so, it is because I have served as the pastor of various sizes of churches. I try to help all of our churches know that they are valuable, regardless of their size or location.

3. Recently I spent some time with the Conference Youth Council (and was made an honorary member!). One of the pastors who works with our Youth Council told me that I am "a youth pastor at heart." I enjoy being with youth, and appreciate their sense of enthusiasm, creativity, and joy. As I get older, I hope that I can continue to be "a youth minister at heart."

4. Two different laymen recently told me that I am an "approachable bishop" to the laity of our conference. I suppose that is easier for me (and for us) because we are a relatively small conference, but I deeply appreciate that observation, and I hope that I can live up to it. I believe it is so important for leaders (like bishops) to be available and accessible. Sometimes I am frustrated by the immense size of the Dakotas, which makes it difficult for me to be very many places quickly. But I guess the issue is to be "approachable" to people wherever I am.

5. Lots of people have told me that I am a "preaching bishop." I love to preach, and I enjoy preaching nearly every Sunday in the churches of our conference. I am not the greatest preacher in the world, but I do believe it is important for people to know and to hear their bishop preach the good news of the gospel.

These various images serve as a challenge, as a goal toward which I stretch, and as a call for my ministry to grow. However, I recently received a new image for my role as a bishop that really surprised me.

My secretary, Naomi Bartle, noted that the General Council on Finance and Administration (GCFA) of our denomination (the group that is literally the employer of all United Methodist bishops) has me insured with the North Dakota Workers Compensation under the label of "Traveling Representative/Salesman." I suppose this label was the closest thing they could find to identify my work as a bishop, but I never quite thought of myself as a "Traveling Representative/Salesman."

The first part of that label does make sense. Bishops and district superintendents are called to travel among the churches and to embody our connectional system. I certainly do travel a lot, and I guess that a bishop is a traveling representative of our denomination. And I hope that I am a good representative of our United Methodist people as I travel among them.

But, what about that "salesman" part? That has led me to reflect upon the question, "What am I selling?" For me, the answer is this: I am not out there traveling around to "sell" the denomination or the conference. I am proudly a United Methodist, and I love serving here in the Dakotas; but I am not a salesman for the institution of The United Methodist Church. Nor am I selling our apportionment or appointment system. It is true that I spend some time trying to interpret and explain this system we use for ministry and for clergy placement, but I don't think of myself as "selling" apportionments or our appointment system.

So, what am I selling? HOPE. I believe that the good news of Jesus Christ is a message of hope and that hope is something that needs to be shared. I believe that I am called (and sent) as a bishop to share a hopeful word with our churches, with our

pastors, with our laity, and with our whole conference. If I have anything with me as I travel, it is
HOPE.

Of course, the hope of the gospel is not for sale;
it is freely given and must be freely received. So, I
am not "selling" hope; but it is the commodity that
I carry with me in my travels. Hope is also the commodity that is refreshed as I visit our pastors and
churches and see the ministry-in-action that is
occurring here in the Dakotas. In other words, I
don't just bring the hope with me, I also receive it as
I get the opportunity to see the ministry of the
United Methodist people here in the Dakotas. So,
maybe I am not really "selling" hope, or even "bringing" hope; I am simply a messenger who learns the
hopeful stories in one part of the Dakotas and
shares them in other parts of this land.

Being a bishop is a lot of things, I am learning,
and it is a great privilege to be a bearer of hope.

And so I pray:

O LORD,
Thank you for providing us with HOPE,
For giving us a reason for ministering and for living;
Thank you for filling our lives with peace and
*   promise,*
For that is the message our churches are giving.

HOPE it is that makes life worth living,
HOPE it is that gives us a direction and a path;
HOPE bring us light when life seems so dark,
HOPE keeps us from falling into the pit of wrath.

Thanks for the privilege of sharing your HOPE,
Thanks for the chance to receive and to share;
Help us to be people who live in your HOPE,
Help us to share your HOPE with people every-
where.

AMEN.

KISSING PIGS AND OTHER STRATEGIES FOR GROWTH

I do it all for the sake of the gospel, so that I may share in its blessings. (1 Corinthians 9:23)

I preached at our United Methodist Church in Dickinson, North Dakota, last month, and I was able to get out of town without having to kiss any pigs.

Let me explain.

Dickinson, North Dakota, is a town of around fifteen thousand population located on I-94 just about sixty miles from the Montana border, making it one of the largest communities in that part of the state. Our United Methodist church there is a lively, growing congregation with a very creative pastor named Kevin Kloster.

Last spring Kevin challenged his congregation to raise extra money for missions, with the promise that he would kiss a pig if they reached the goal. Of course the people responded to that challenge, and Kevin faced the task of finding a pig to kiss. A pig was selected, and Kevin announced that he would visit the pig a few times before the fateful Sunday, because he "didn't think it would be right to kiss a pig on their first date."

To everyone's surprise, and Kevin's embarrassment, the pig died before that Sunday arrived! This, of course, led to much talk around town that the pig would rather die than to have to kiss the United Methodist pastor!

However, another pig was located, and Kevin announced that the pig-kissing would occur on the Sunday that the congregation was to vote on purchasing an additional parking lot. Of course this provided a large crowd on that Sunday (and proved the point about needing to purchase additional space for parking). After the worship service concluded the pig-kissing event began. Kevin brought flowers to the pig and placed a grape in his own lips for the pig to retrieve—and thus the "kiss." Naturally he had to repeat this several times, so that everyone got a chance to take a picture of the "kiss." It was quite a day.

This fall I was invited to preach at Dickinson United Methodist Church on their Homecoming Sunday, which was also announced as the Sunday to finish their drive to pay for the new parking lot. Having the bishop present and having Homecoming Sunday (complete with a special meal and musical entertainment) also produced a nice crowd—to remind people of the need to pay for the new parking lot. Fortunately the day's festivities did not include any pig-kissing.

So, that is the story of how one pastor here in the Dakotas developed a growth strategy around kissing a pig. It might not be the right strategy for everyone, and it certainly required the approval of Kevin's understanding wife, Tracy; but it worked for Dickinson Church. The principles seem pretty sound: create some interest, set some clear goals, and have a little fun with the whole process.

I'm just glad that I didn't have to kiss the pig, aren't you?

And so I pray:

O LORD,
How great it is to have fun with church,
Instead of making it too dreary and serious.
The idea of church being boring and cold
Leaves us with no joy or sense of the mysterious.

It is great to set goals, and to move toward those
    goals
With almost reckless abandon;
Knowing all the while that our mission and task
Must always be planned and not just random.

So, keep us from taking our ministry too seriously,
Help us to laugh and to try some new things;
Give us some joy along with our hard work
And help us to let celebration take wing.

Even pigs are a part of your kingdom,
And pig-kissing can be a part of it all;
So thanks for the chance to join in your mission,
And let us have fun as we follow your call.
                                                AMEN.

DON'T FORGET FIRST BASE

But strive first for the kingdom of God and his right-eousness, and all these things will be given to you as well.

(Matthew 6:33)

*W*here were you when Mark McGwire hit home run sixty-two and broke the record set by Roger Maris who hit sixty-one in 1961? Did you see the excitement that was produced in St. Louis and around the country? Were you watching something else on TV, only to have your viewing interrupted by a special news report about McGwire's homer? Were you impressed by the attitude of the young man who found that famous baseball and who modestly insisted that it belonged to McGwire (instead of selling it to a collector for a large sum of money)? Didn't Mark McGwire show a lot of class by greeting the widow and family of Roger Maris (who has never gotten the credit he deserved for breaking Babe Ruth's record of sixty home runs)?

It was a great event, and if you enjoy sports at all then you had to enjoy watching Mark McGwire hit that famous home run.

In the midst of it all, I finally noticed one more

---

thing on the 189th replay of that home run: namely, that Mark almost forgot to touch first base as he made his triumphant run around the bases. He was so excited, that his first base coach literally had to grab him and remind him to touch first base as he went by. Otherwise, the rules of baseball say that he would have been out! Wouldn't that have been tragic and controversial?

Yet life is like that—we must touch "first base" before moving on to anything else. In every avenue of life there are certain basics, certain beginning points, certain fundamentals that must be "touched" before we can ever score a "home run."

Recently I was talking with a pastor in our Dakotas Conference who complained to me, "Our local church just can't seem to keep the main thing as the main thing." He further explained, "We seem to talk about fund-raising, rather than talking about stewardship. We focus upon membership, rather than focusing upon making disciples. We talk about social events, but not about deeper kinds of fellowship and caring. We are always missing the main point and getting sidetracked on less important issues."

I don't know whether his assessment is correct, but I believe he is on to something very important. In everything we do in life, there are basics, core values, and central issues that must be our focus. Otherwise, everything else we do is unimportant. It is so easy to become distracted from the main thing and to waste our time and energy on secondary issues.

I heard of another church in another part of the country that spent over two years planning to do an evangelism program. They studied, talked, planned, produced charts, evaluated, and wrote

position papers. After two years they finally produced an evangelism plan that had thirty-seven
priorities! About that same time, there was a pastoral change at that church, and a year later they
received over one hundred new members. How did
that happen? It wasn't the plan. The new pastor
simply focused his time and energy upon responding to newcomers who were already attending that
church. He didn't need a planning document, he
just responded to people's needs and invited them
to become a part of the church.

Now, planning has its place, and using the com-
bined wisdom of a ministry team or committee can
be helpful. But when we depart from the main
thing and spend all our time in planning, sometimes we never get around to actually doing the
main thing.

What is the main thing or the "first base" in your
life and ministry? Perhaps you and your church
need to focus on discovering God's vision and purpose. Perhaps you need to stop talking about side
issues and start dealing with the central core of our
Christian faith. Perhaps you keep skipping over the
first step of helping your people become better disciples, and you are trying to rush on to getting people involved in too many other things. Perhaps your
worship service is too filled with announcements
and fellowship, and you need to provide more
opportunities to focus on celebrating the presence
of God. Perhaps it is easy to miss "first base" when
we are trying so hard to hit home runs.

Mark McGwire's story reminds us that home
runs do happen, new levels of excellence do occur,
and great effort does bring great results. His story
also reminds us not to miss first base. I hope you
score some home runs this week, but it probably

won't happen unless you touch first base along the way.

And so I pray:

O Lord,
Help us to keep before us what is most important,
Remind us of your values and priorities;
It is so easy to get distracted by those lesser things
In the midst of all our busy responsibilities.

Home runs do happen, and our ministries produce results,
Sometimes when we least expect;
Yet too often when we get sidetracked or confused,
Too often we can overlook or neglect.

First base is always the start of the journey,
Finding out what is first and keeping it there;
Otherwise we can skip and miss what is most important
And find ourselves making quite an error.

AMEN.

WHEN IS
A CHRISTIAN?

Not everyone who says to me, "Lord, Lord," will enter the kingdom of heaven, but only the one who does the will of my Father in heaven. (Matthew 7:21)

---

*T*here seems to be a lot of debate these days about "What is a Christian?" These debates turn toward defining what is "true" belief or doctrine, sometimes even going into issues of "purity of belief" (whatever that means). There are those who argue that being a Christian is more than just following Jesus; it must also involve having the right set of beliefs about Jesus and being able to articulate those beliefs with all of the right language.

I tend to believe that the more important question may be, *"When* is a Christian?" I believe that a Christian is more clearly defined by the behaviors we exhibit, rather what beliefs or doctrines or concepts we say that we believe. In simple terms this is often expressed around the Dakotas as, "You've got to walk the walk, not just talk the talk." Two recent experiences may help illustrate this.

Last month while I was in San Francisco for a meeting, I spent a day visiting Glide Memorial United Methodist Church. Glide is a unique United Methodist church, ministering in the "ten-

---

derloin district" of San Francisco, an area of great poverty, drug use, violence, and crime. Glide Church does some amazing ministry, including a huge project of feeding the homeless of the area three meals a day, seven days a week. Many of the other ministries of Glide Church are way outside of my own comfort zone, including their huge ministry to the gay and lesbian community of San Francisco. The style used by Glide is unique in its ministry, too, and it is not a style that is readily copied elsewhere.

What impressed me most about the experience at Glide was their clear sense of "doing" ministry and the results of that doing. During my visit, I sat next to a young woman named Angel who talked of being a drug addict and prostitute for seventeen years before Glide Church helped her to get clean and to stay clean. The church helped her get an education, and she is now one of the counselors in their anti-drug–addiction programs. No matter what anyone thinks about the theology or worship style of Glide, it is hard to argue with its results!

Just recently I heard from one of our pastors about a typical story of "doing ministry" here in the Dakotas. She reported that a farmer in his early fifties died suddenly in her community, and now the neighboring farmers will be pitching in to help the family with the fall harvest routine. Our pastor said, "That family has not been very regular churchgoers, but that didn't matter to our people. They are willing to help, and I know this will have a major impact on that family, and upon our entire community." I am sure that it will.

Stories like Angel's and the farming community's are the best definitions of being a Christian. A Christian is not just someone who professes belief in the right doctrines, or someone who uses the right words to describe his or her relationship to Christ, or someone who has the best knowledge of Scripture. No, a person is a Christian when he or she acts like a follower of Jesus Christ by loving, caring, healing, proclaiming, sharing, and giving in the manner of Christ—"walking the walk" and not just "talking the talk."

Now, don't get me wrong. I am not against learning to talk about the walk. I have two theological degrees, and I believe in the importance of faith seeking understanding. We must help people who are walking the walk to talk about their walk in a way that helps others know about the journey of following Christ.

But the walking comes first. Jesus invited his followers to "Come, follow me," and he sent out disciples long before they fully understood his message and mission. Jesus seems to have a bias for action, for feeding hungry people and healing sick people. Jesus in the Gospels sometimes ends up having to argue religious language with the Pharisees and other religious leaders, but it seems obvious that his preference is to serve, to care, to proclaim, to heal, and to love. And it is also obvious that Jesus calls us to be his followers by joining with him in this ministry. When we do that, then we are truly Christian.

And so I pray:

O LORD, Teach us how to follow Jesus along the way,
Not just in our words but also in our deeds;

Show us how to be a disciple who cares and shares
And responds to others in need.

Following Christ is not just a mental exercise,
Following Christ is more than just talk;
So help us to put our faith into action,
And take our discipleship for a walk.

AMEN.

No More Violence

Above all, clothe yourselves with love, which binds everything together in perfect harmony. And let the peace of Christ rule in your hearts, to which indeed you were called in the one body. And be thankful.

(Colossians 3:14-15)

Matthew Shepard died in our neighboring state of Wyoming. He was a young, gay man (a freshman at the University of Wyoming) who was the victim of violence and hatred against homosexual persons. According to news reports, two men seized Matthew, robbed him, beat him nearly to death, tied him to a fence post like a scarecrow, and left him for dead. He was found by passersby and taken to a hospital where he lingered for a few days and then died. Two men have been arrested, and it seems likely that their two girlfriends will also be arrested for assisting in this ghastly crime.

As I look at a map and see how close Wyoming is to the Dakotas Area where I serve (bordering on the western edge of South Dakota), I am sickened with the thought of how nearby this unthinkable crime occurred.

How can anyone hate another person enough to

do that kind of violence? Is our fear of homosexual persons so great that it leads people to act in such inhuman ways? Why is it that some heterosexual persons can only feel "tough" by expressing their hatred toward homosexual men and women?

This terrible news event from our neighboring state makes me wonder about the current debate in our United Methodist denomination over the issue of homosexuality. Somewhere in the midst of this significant debate and its related topics of scriptural authority, the role of church tradition, medical evidence, and personal experience, have we as a denomination sent any false signals that would allow anyone to think that hatred of homosexual persons is ever acceptable? Certainly our Social Principles state boldly that "homosexual persons are persons of sacred worth," and we are called to be engaged in ministry with and to homosexual persons. Yet still I wonder, has all of this debate given anyone the idea that we would ever condone violence against gay and lesbian persons?

I hope not. But I have to report that some of the mail that I receive about this issue (especially from elsewhere in the country) is filled with hatred. In the midst of an important debate in our denomination, there are some really crazy-sounding people who get involved and spread hatred and fear and threats and accusations.

So let all of us, no matter where we stand on the debate about homosexuality, affirm again—in as bold a way as we can—that violence against any person because of his or her sexual preferences or practices is always wrong. Let there be NO MORE VIOLENCE against the Matthew Shepards of the world, or against anyone else. NO MORE VIOLENCE.

And so I pray:

O Lord,
How awful it is to know that violence and evil are
    present
In our world in strange and powerful ways;
I suppose that such evil deeds and prejudice are
    always around
Trying to cast their ignorant sway.

Save us from hatred and violence toward one
    another,
Help us treat each one as a sister or brother.
Never let us imply in all of our rhetoric
That such violence is anything but totally pathetic.

Forgive us for our part in spreading such hatred,
Forgive us for not stopping or objecting to its use;
Keep us from condoning by our words or our silence
Such evil prejudice, violence, and abuse.

Amen.

*U*FFDA!

*B*ut *where sin increased, grace abounded all the more.*

(Romans 5:20)

*U*p in this part of the Dakotas there are lots of Norwegians and other folks who use the phrase, *Uffda!* I have come to appreciate this phrase, and I would propose that it be added to any serious theological document produced by the church.

Uffda! is one of those words that is difficult to translate. It could mean, "Oh, no!" but it is even stronger than that. It might be translated, "Oops!" if that word were any more clear in its meaning. Sometimes *Uffda!* is a replacement for a curse, sometimes it is a gentle phrase for "Uh-oh," and sometimes it is an expression that combines anger, humor, and frustration all at once.

A greeting card I found in the Fargo airport gift shop contains some of the following translations of *Uffda!*:

- Uffda! *is what you say when you look into the mirror and realize that you are not getting better, you are just getting older.*
- Uffda! *is what you say when you drop your chew-*

*ing gum in the chicken lot and find it three differ-
ent times.*
- Uffda! *is what you feel when you realize that they
aren't laughing with you, they are laughing at you.*

I believe that *Uffda!* is an important theological
concept that might be translated: "We are all
human," or even "Life is fragile," or possibly "Sin is
real." Maybe the scriptural reference for *Uffda!*
would be in Romans 5:20 (although it must be
noted that the limitations of the Greek and Hebrew
languages of the original Scripture texts resulted in
the unfortunate omission of *Uffda!* from our
Bibles). In that verse, Paul (who must have been at
least partly Norwegian) says, "Where sin increased,
grace abounded all the more." For, you see, *Uffda!*
is actually an expression of grace.

Whenever someone makes a mistake, drops and
breaks a prized possession, forgets an important
detail, utters a less-than-wise comment, or commits any other human error, all that person has to
do is utter *Uffda!* and all is forgiven. *Uffda!* is the
ultimate expression of grace. It means, "I goofed,
I'm sorry, and I know that my mistake is just part
of the praxis of our human existence" (well, actually
no self-respecting Norwegian would use the word
praxis). Then the appropriate response by everyone
else is a polite chuckle and a theologically correct
word of grace and forgiveness as they repeat the
offender's comment by replying, *"Uffda!"* Once
Uffda! is repeated, everyone knows that the issue is
forgotten, forgiven, and settled. It is simply another
case of *Uffda!*—a sample of our human sin that is
covered by God's amazing grace.

It is also important to follow the unwritten rules
of *Uffda!* etiquette. Sometimes people try to engage

in *Uffda!*-upsmanship by stating *Uffda!* to another person to point out his or her mistake. That is never proper. *Uffda!* must be stated first by the offender; then others respond with their own statement of *Uffda!* The expression *Uffda!* must never be used as a put-down or in a judgmental tone to one who has committed an *Uffda!* No, *Uffda!* always begins, appropriately, as an act of confession, which is followed by others who repeat *Uffda!* as the response of forgiveness and reconciliation.

By now you can probably tell that I am almost serious that *Uffda!* should be in our theological vocabulary. We don't all have to be Norwegians (and I know some of you are grateful for that fact), but we do all stand in need of grace—God's grace, most importantly, but also some words of grace from one another. Or as the Norwegians up here say it, *Uffda!*

And so I pray (and sing):

Amazing Uffda! *How sweet the sound*
That saved a wretch like me!
I once was lost, but now am found,
Was blind, but now I see.

'Twas Uffda! *that taught my heart to fear,*
And Uffda! *my fears relieved;*
How precious did that Uffda! *appear*
The hour I first believed.

Through many dangers, toils, and snares,
I have already come;
'Tis Uffda! *hath brought me safe thus far,*
And Uffda! *will lead me home.*

                                        Amen.

THE FIRST SNOW

I also know that you are enduring patiently and bearing up for the sake of my name, and that you have not grown weary. But I have this against you, that you have abandoned the love you had at first. (Revelation 2:3-4)

By the beginning of November just about every part of the Dakotas Area has received its First Snow of the winter. I was in Rapid City, South Dakota, just in time for their first ten inches or so of the season. A few days later in Fargo we were blessed with our first snowstorm and the first day of school missed already. Sioux Falls, South Dakota, got hit the hardest in the last few days, including "thunder snow" with both lightning and snowstorms to go with wind gusts up to sixty miles per hour. I have heard from our district superintendent in the northwest district who has already been snowed in for a few days in a motel during his charge conference rounds.

So, yes, I can state with conviction: we have had our First Snow of the season here in the Dakotas.

First Snow is different from all of the others. People wait in anticipation of the First Snow, asking each other with some expectation but also with anxiety, "Have you had your First Snow yet?" People also seem to use the First Snow of the season as a time to re-learn about driving on snow and ice, and I believe that First Snow must be just about the most dangerous time to drive in the Dakotas. It is as though everyone has never seen snow before, and they drive like it was still dry pavement and warm weather.

First Snow also brings with it a sense of wonder and awe. Seeing the world transformed by the beauty of First Snow is awesome indeed. Last weekend as I drove around the Black Hills of southwest South Dakota and observed the Ponderosa pine trees (whose black-colored bark gives the Black Hills their name) covered evenly with a thick blanket of wet snow, I was lost in a moment of appreciation for the beauty of it all.

First Snow often brings with it a sense of neighboring, as people go outside to shovel and plow their driveways and streets together. Children are out playing in the First Snow, making the first snowmen of the season. Adults even seem to enjoy the chance to get out in the First Snow of the season.

All of that changes after First Snow becomes Still Snow. By the fourth, or eighth, or fourteenth snowstorm of the season, all of the beauty, joy, and awe of First Snow will be replaced by the anger, frustration, and disgust of Still Snow as we wonder how long this winter will last.

Why is First Snow is so different from Still Snow? I don't know, but I think it is a phenomenon much like First Love, or First Car, or First-Day-of-a-New-Job. We humans tend to get excited about the new and different, but then quickly take for granted that which used to be new and now is the same-old-thing.

It is even true with our Christian faith and ministry. John writes to the church at Ephesus this haunting accusation: "I have this against you, that you have abandoned the love you had at first" (Revelation 2:4). It is an accusation that could be leveled against many of us, as we start to take for granted our experience of God's gracious love. That is why it is so healthy for churches to have a constant flow of new Christians into their midst—those who are afresh with an experience of God's grace and forgiveness, those who are filled with a sense of gratitude for God's love, those who are filled with First Love. The rest of us long-time veterans of the faith can too easily fall into the Still Christian syndrome of a faith without freshness and newness.

I hope that First Snow will not turn too quickly into Still Snow. I trust that my early enthusiasm for ministry will grow and mature without becoming flat and dull. I hope that all of our Dakotas churches will be filled with First Love Christians no matter how many years they have been on the faith journey.

And I pray:

O Lord,
Whose love is new every morning,
O Lord, whose Word is alive and fresh every day,
Keep us filled with your newness and your grace,
And guide us into new paths along the way.

Keep us from becoming stale and stagnant in our
_   faith;_
Keep us from falling into the same old ruts;

Teach us to have a faith that is eager and bold;
Fill us with courage and with guts.

The First Snow of winter has come upon us,
Leading some to expect a season so drear;
But remind us that First Snow and First Love
Can show us that New Love is always here.

AMEN.

HAVE A SEAT

Do not neglect to show hospitality to strangers, for by doing that some have entertained angels without knowing it.   *(Hebrews 13:2)*

-----

*O*ur newest congregation in the Dakotas Conference, Friendship United Methodist Church in Fargo, is in the process of constructing their first building. They anticipate being in their first unit by February or March, and of course they are excited about finally moving out of the school where they have worshiped since 1993.

As anyone who has moved into a new house, new office, or new church building can attest, there will be many needs for the Friendship congregation once they are in their new building. In order to help them, and also to give all of our churches a chance to support this new congregation, our Conference Council on Finance and Administration has approved a special request to all of our churches: to purchase a chair for the Friendship church all-purpose room where they will have their worship services and other activities. Each chair will cost about forty dollars, and a letter will be coming soon to each of our churches asking them to purchase one or more chairs for Friendship Church. They

-----

will need 220 chairs. We have 180 charges in the Dakotas Conference, so it would be great to have every church or charge purchase at least one chair as an act of solidarity with our newest congregation. In order to get the process started, the district superintendents and I will each purchase a chair for Friendship Church.

All of which reminds me of an experience I had several years ago in Indiana. I was visiting and having dinner in one of the parsonages of my district, when I noticed that the parsonage family had one extra seat and place setting at their dinner table. When I inquired about this, they responded that it was a part of their family tradition to always have one extra seat at their table—to remind them to be prepared for any guest who might arrive. They said to me, "No matter who shows up at our table for dinner, even if it be Christ himself, we want to be prepared and able to say, 'You are welcome here, have a seat!' "

As we head into the Thanksgiving and Christmas seasons, it is my prayer that all of us will practice such hospitality in our homes and in our churches. Hebrews 13:2 reminds us, "Do not neglect to show hospitality to strangers, for by so doing that some have entertained angels without knowing it." We provide hospitality by the attitude with which we welcome newcomers and visitors in our midst. We provide hospitality by the way we speak to strangers and treat them like guests. And we provide hospitality by the provisions we make to have enough seats and space for those who come to our doors.

Maybe helping to purchase a chair for our newest church is another good way to practice hospitality. It certainly is a good way to say, "You are welcome here—have a seat!"

And so I pray:

O LORD,
Thank you for making a place for us at your table;
You have welcomed us into your kingdom and your
  family.
Help us to be welcoming, too, and help us to make
Our churches ready to receive any company.

Strangers are guests and friends we have not yet
  known;
Newcomers are people who need to be received;
So help us to welcome and to greet with rejoicing
Everyone who comes and seeks to believe.

No one is ever excluded from your grace,
And no one should be excluded from your kin.
So make our churches places of openness
Where strangers are welcomed again and again.

AMEN.

LESSONS
FROM THE GRINCH

Sing praises to the Lord, O you his faithful ones,

and give thanks to his holy name.

For his anger is but for a moment;

his favor is for a lifetime.

Weeping may linger for the night,

but joy comes with the morning.

(Psalm 30:4-5)

---

*I*n early December we visited Bishop and Mrs. John Hopkins in Minneapolis. John and Elaine are long-time friends from Indiana, and in fact John and I were in the same elders ordination class in the North Indiana Conference. John later was transferred to the South Indiana Conference, and he and I were both elected on the same ballot at the 1996 Jurisdictional Conference. So Marsha and I enjoyed having a chance to visit with them, and we also went to see their residence, the bishop's office, and some of the downtown Minneapolis decorations for Christmas.

We even attended the downtown Christmas parade, and then we went through the Christmas display at Dayton's department store. This year's display was about the wonderful Dr. Seuss book, *How the Grinch Stole Christmas.* It was fun to see the display and to watch the faces of the many children going through the display with us.

Christmas storybooks have some very adult messages, too. It has been a long time since I have had the chance to read the Grinch book to a child, so I had forgotten some of the messages. In case you don't have a little one to read to, or in case you have forgotten, here are some of the messages of that so-called children's book:

- The Grinch is jealous of other people enjoying Christmas because he has a heart that is "two sizes too small."
- The Grinch decides to steal everyone's Christmas presents, their decorations, and even their Christmas trees so that he can have Christmas all to himself.
- The Grinch is surprised to discover that the people (called the "Whos") are still able to celebrate Christmas, even without their gifts and decorations.
- The Grinch further discovers that Christmas isn't just about gifts, decorations, and trees, it is about "something more."
- The Grinch's heart suddenly grows several sizes, he returns all of the Christmas items to the Whos, and he is invited to join them in celebrating Christmas.

Not a bad list of lessons to learn at this time of year, is it? Not just a book for kids, is it? It is even something a preacher could preach about, isn't it?

How about you? Is your heart "two sizes too

small"? Do you need to let your heart grow several sizes this Christmas? Do you know that Christmas is "something more" than just presents, gifts, decorations, church programs, and even worship services?

Merry Christmas to all . . . to all the children of all ages . . . and to all the Grinches, too!

And so I pray:

O LORD,
Stretch our hearts; stretch them during these Christmas days,
Take away our cheapness, and fill us with your generous ways.

Stretch our minds, Lord, stretch them during this Christmas season,
Take away our old thoughts, and fill us with your gracious reason.

Stretch our love, Lord, stretch us during this Christmas celebration,
Take away our sorrows, and fill us with your jubilation.

Stretch our lives, Lord, stretch us during this Christmas time,
Take away our failures, and start on us the upward climb.

Stretch our churches, Lord, stretch them during this Christmas joy,
Take away our smallness, and help us share this baby boy.

AMEN.

CHECK THIS OUT

---

*H*onest balances and scales are the LORD's;

all the weights in the bag are his work.

(Proverbs 16:11)

---

*O*ne thing that continually amazes me here in the Dakotas is the way people write checks for nearly everything. Standing in line at a gas station, paying at a check-out in a hardware store, dealing with a cashier in a restaurant—almost everywhere in the Dakotas I see people paying with a personal check. And—this is what really amazes me—I almost never see any cashier ask for any proof of identity! How can that be?

Everywhere else I have lived or traveled, checks are suspect. Merchants are far more likely to welcome credit cards than checks. Here in the Dakotas, I have been many places where credit cards are not accepted, but the merchant will gladly accept a personal check. That is sometimes a problem for me, since my wife carries our checkbook. I usually have a little cash, but I rely upon debit cards and credit cards, especially since I usually need a receipt to verify my expenditures. So imagine my surprise when my attempts to pay with a credit card or debit card have been greeted with,

---

"I'm sorry. We don't accept those, but we would be glad to take your check." What is going on here? How can checks be more welcome than credit cards?

I discussed this recently with Bishop Rick Foss, who is the Lutheran (Evangelical Lutheran Church in America) bishop in eastern North Dakota. We have lunch on a somewhat regular basis, since we both live in Fargo and we have similar ministry positions. I think that Rick explained this "check" situation better than anyone else I have encountered. Here is what he said:

• Dakotas people are honest.
• Merchants frown upon credit cards because they believe being in debt is bad.

Could it really be that simple? Do people in the Dakotas have a basic sense of trust and honesty that makes personal checks a safe way to give/receive payment? Is a check more like cash (real money), whereas a credit card is associated with paying later?

I believe it may be that simple. It is also similar to the common practice in the Dakotas of *not locking* one's house or one's car. People trust people. People are basically honest. People don't steal (our crime rate is very low, and it seems to be more than just our cold weather). People know that someone's word (or check) is good. People believe that what other people say (and pay) will be "right."

Recently one of our new pastors told me that when he and his family went on a vacation, they decided they should lock the parsonage while they were away. The only problem was, no one (including all the trustees in the church) could remember when or where they had last seen any keys for the house! So, they went on vacation with the house unlocked as usual. Did anyone get into the house while they were gone, I asked? Oh yes, he said. The people of his parish came in and stocked the refrigerator with some fresh supplies the day before the pastoral family returned, because the parishioners didn't want them to be without the basics upon their return. While they were in the parsonage, they also vacuumed and dusted a little.

My own experience is similar. I have stayed in motels in small communities in the Dakotas (usually on my way to preach at one of our parishes) where the message from the proprietor when my secretary made the reservation was something like this: "We don't stay up very late, so if he gets here after 8 P.M. he can just find the key to his room on the counter inside the motel office."

Experiences like that make it easier to understand why a lot of people in the Dakotas don't lock their houses. It also explains why someone's personal check is regarded as "good" until proven otherwise.

Don't get me wrong—people in the Dakotas are not naive or stupid. They soon figure out who is trustworthy and who is not. In our larger communities (like here in Fargo) most people probably do lock their cars and their houses, and we do have some crime. But here is the difference from other places where I have lived and served: people in the Dakotas start with a basic assumption of trust and honesty. They are disappointed when people prove to be dishonest, but they don't start out by mistrusting people or expecting anyone's check to be bad. They start from a position of trust in the basic honesty of human beings, and for the most part they are not disappointed.

I read somewhere that people usually live and

act the way we treat them. In fact, Harvard University did a study entitled *The Pygmalion Effect* (named after the stage play from which *My Fair Lady* was produced) in which they discovered that students usually achieve just about the level that their teachers expect of them. Maybe believing the best about people, trusting people, expecting honesty, and assuming that a person's word is good— maybe that helps to create a climate in which people actually live and act with honesty and integrity. I don't know if it could work in Washington, DC, but it seems to work that way here in the Dakotas. And I am grateful for it, but I sure wish everyone would accept my credit cards, too.

And so I pray:

O LORD,
Keep us honest and trusting,
And keep us worthy of such trust from others;
Give us a faithfulness that uplifts
Rather than a mistrust that smothers.

Let our word be our truth, O Lord,
Just like your Word is Truth for us.
Help us to know what is right and to do it,
Without excuses, lies, or fuss.

A check is just a piece of paper,
Behind it lies the trust that gives it value;
So it must be with our lives and our faith,
Where trust is our only sure avenue.

AMEN.

REMOTE-STARTING THE CHURCH

*P*ray *without ceasing.*

(1 Thessalonians 5:17)

*F*or Christmas last year my dad gave me a remote starter for my car. He wanted to help me survive another harsh Dakota winter, so he gave me an Auto Command System that starts my car by remote control from as far away as five hundred feet. The idea is to stay inside my house or office or motel, start the car by remote control to let it warm up, and then go outside and get into a nice warm car. It is a great system, and I have been using it regularly.

Of course this device has led to some interesting situations. Oftentimes I find people standing around my car, peering into the windows, trying to figure out how the car started by itself. Recently I found two older women standing next to my car, staring at it, and having a discussion. I assumed that they were really impressed by this new technology, but instead I overheard them saying to each other, "Some poor idiot left his car running with the keys locked inside." In spite of the evaluation of those two women, I really appreciate this remote-starting opportunity.

Which has led me to wonder: How do we remote-start the church? I have noticed many churches that seem almost lifeless, and then suddenly they spring to life on some issue or some ministry opportunity. They have had worship and fellowship for years, their pastors have preached and served faithfully, and their laity have been loyal church members. But suddenly something happens and the whole church comes to life. How does that happen?

Wouldn't it be great to have a remote starter for our churches? I have even fantasized about sitting in the bishop's office in Fargo, looking at the map that displays the locations of all our churches, and pushing some kind of remote starter and . . . presto! One or more of those churches would become more alive and vital than it has ever been!

From some of the correspondence I receive, there must be lots of United Methodists who believe that we bishops possess such a device. Unfortunately, if there is such a thing in my office, I have not yet located it.

Let me suggest an alternative. I believe that the Holy Spirit remote-starts the church and that the "device" is prayer. Every church I know that has had an experience of sudden life or new birth has done so because of significant prayer by its pastors and lay leaders. It is through prayer that we make ourselves available to the power of God's Spirit to give our churches (and us as individuals) the remote start that we need. Through prayer we provide an access for the Spirit to give us new life.

I envision every church having a group of laity who pray for their pastor just before he or she leads them in worship. Every pastor gets inundated with announcements, last-minute schedule changes, and other sorts of information overload before worship services begin. These things make it difficult for pastors to be spiritually prepared to lead the services. Wouldn't it be great for a group of the laity of the church to gather the pastor in a prayer circle and to ask God to empower their pastor to lead them in worship?

I envision every church having a prayer group that meets at least weekly to pray for the concerns and needs of the church and the community. It is important for such groups to avoid being gossip groups, because then they could help to remote-start God's healing presence in the lives of individuals and churches. Such groups are often stronger and more vital when they are led by laity and the pastor can attend as a participant.

I envision every United Methodist in the Dakotas (laity and clergy) taking time each day to pray and to ask God to help our churches to be alive to God's presence. What might happen if these forty-eight thousand Christians prayed daily for God to remote-start our churches? We might find people peering into our windows (and walking into our doors) to discover how our churches suddenly came to life.

That's my dream. Every time I remote-start my car I also pray for God's Spirit to remote-start me, our pastors, and our churches.

And so I pray:

———

O LORD,
Get us started, and make us alive and anew.
Remote-start us with the gift of the Spirit that comes
from you. Don't let us sit idly by, don't let us simply

———

go through the motions. Start us with your great spiritual power, and set us all into motion.

Too long we have waited and not seemed alive; too often we have missed opportunities to serve. Give us your power and make us alive; fill us with your strength and your verve.

We are open and waiting, ready to hear when you say, "Today is the day to be more alive, to be led anew in my ways." So fill us with your Spirit and teach us always to pray, that we and our churches may be more alive to your way.

AMEN.

CELEBRATING SMALL SUCCESSES

Rejoice in the Lord always; again I will say, Rejoice. . . .
I know what it is to have little, and I know what it is to
have plenty. . . . I can do all things through him who
strengthens me. (Philippians 4:4, 12a, 13)

*H*ow do you measure success? Sometimes it is as simple as tying your own shoes. While we were visiting family in Indiana over the holidays, my father-in-law proudly showed us how he had learned to tie his own shoes. It was wonderful to see the joy on his face as he celebrated this success.

You see, Howard had a stroke on Labor Day weekend four years ago. For a while we thought he would not live, and then we were concerned that he might be totally paralyzed and never talk or understand again. After a long recovery, he can walk now (with a severe limp). He can understand everything that is said to him, but his impaired speech requires considerable patience for us to converse with him. His right arm has slowly regained strength and dexterity, and so with a great deal of practice in recent weeks he has relearned how to tie his own shoes. It is a great accomplishment, and we all celebrated with him.

Great big successes are easy to celebrate, but it is perhaps even more important to celebrate the small successes that require so much effort. As we reflect on our lives, it helps to remember and to celebrate the small successes. To get started with the celebration, here is a list of questions about your recent successes:

- Did you make a new friend, or renew an old friendship?
- Did you take time to give a special gift to someone in need, above your usual gift-giving?
- Did you read your Bible and have devotional times more this year than previous years?
- Did your church welcome new members last year and help them to feel at home?
- Did you provide for your family this past year, at least in terms of their needs?
- Did your church faithfully have worship services every Sunday and every special season?
- Did you learn any new lessons about life this past year?
- Did you tell everyone whom you love that you love them? Did you tell them often?
- Did your church sponsor any events to help the children of your community?
- Did your church sponsor any events to help the poor of your community?
- Did your church have any special celebrations, anniversaries, or just plain fun times this past year?
- Did your family spend some time together on a vacation or doing some event that was worth taking pictures of and remembering?
- Did you forgive anyone this past year who really didn't deserve being forgiven?
- Were you forgiven this past year when you really didn't deserve it?

- Did you visit anyone who was lonely?
- Did you pray for anyone who needed special prayers?
- Did you take food or clothing or basic necessities to anyone who really needed it?
- Did you thank God for your health and do anything to improve your health?
- Did you grow in your awareness of God's grace?

If you can answer yes to any of these questions, then you have some small successes to celebrate. You have some reasons to look back and say, "It was a good year." You have some things to help you prepare for life in the next year. What is success, anyway? Sometimes it is as simple as tying your own shoes.

And so I pray:

───────────

O LORD,

Thank you for the successes of this past year, not just the major ones that everyone will mention, but also the smaller ones that could go unnoticed, the ones that require our special attention.

We are reminded that your kingdom comes in small ways. It is in the simple things that we show we are your kin, so help us remember the little ways we've been faithful, and remind us to celebrate those victories again.

Lead us into another year with a new sense of your grace, and keep us faithful to you in both big and small ways. Help us to stay faithful and to stay focused on your purpose, and give us strength, even in little things, to follow you always.

AMEN.

───────────

REBUILDING FAITH

Now if anyone builds on the foundation with gold, silver, precious stones, wood, hay, straw—the work of each builder will become visible, for the Day will disclose it, because it will be revealed with fire, and the fire will test what sort of work each has done.

(1 Corinthians 3:12-13)

On December 29, Faith United Methodist Church in Fargo, North Dakota, had a serious fire that gutted its fellowship hall and educational wing. The fire was discovered by a passerby, and the fire department reacted quickly enough to save the church office area and the sanctuary—although both of those areas suffered from heavy smoke and water damage. Fortunately the church had just upgraded their insurance to a full-replacement-value insurance, so the cleaning, rebuilding, and restoration costs should be well covered.

On the Sunday following the fire, which also happened to be the first Sunday of the New Year, the people of Faith Church gathered for worship at a warehouse/reception hall that was offered for their use by a member of their church. I was able to attend that service, and it was an uplifting experience to see the people rally together on that cold Sunday morning. Over 250 persons attended, and the spirit was warm and determined. The congregation sang, "I am the church, you are the church, we are the church together"; the choir (which had practiced at a member's home) sang a seasonal number; and the pastor preached about not asking, "Why us?" but rather accepting that tragedy is part of life and trusting God to help us deal with such times. A member who turned ninety on the day of the fire was recognized, and she added some needed humor to the day by asserting, "It is not true that the fire was caused by lighting all ninety candles on my birthday cake!"

It was a great service, and the fellowship time afterwards was especially nice. Amid camera crews from two local television stations, the people drank coffee, ate birthday cake, were interviewed by the media, and enjoyed being together as the church. All of this supported my own words of greeting to the congregation when I said, "Faith Church did not burn. Your building had a fire, and it will need to be restored. But the church is more than a building, it is the people of God. Seeing you here today for worship reminds me that Faith Church did not burn; it is alive and well."

Those words were not mine. You see, when I was in sixth grade, my home church building in Anderson, Indiana, burned to the ground on the Saturday night before Christmas. Many of our members arrived on Sunday morning to share in the decorations, Christmas carols, and the joy of the season, only to find our church building standing as an eery, ice-covered, burned-out shell. We gathered for a quickly designed worship service in the local high school auditorium, where the pastors and the lay leaders of that congregation asserted boldly, over and over again, "Our church did not burn. Our building burned, but our church is the people of God, and we will go on."

Thus my formative years were spent as a part of a congregation that did not have a building for several years. I saw firsthand that the church is more than a building, and it helped shape my life and my faith. It is probably no coincidence that four of us from the youth group during those rebuilding years are ordained United Methodist clergy today. Somehow having to discover through tragedy that the church is much more than a building also helped us discover God's call into ministry.

So, Faith United Methodist Church in Fargo, North Dakota, did not burn. They had a fire in their building; but the congregation is alive, vital, committed, and determined to continue. They have already established a Website on which you can see pictures of their fire and leave them messages of encouragement and hope. The site is titled, "rebuildfaith"—a great title for a congregation that is responding to a crisis with a faith that will rebuild their building and reaffirm their own faith.

And so I pray:

O Lord,
Thank you for our church buildings, for the witness that they represent. Thank you, Lord, for our properties, for their brick, wood, stone, and cement.
But help us to remember always, O Lord, that the church is so much, much more than brick and mor-

---

tar and walls. Your church is built of the people you
adore.

   Help us to be the people of God, O Lord; the kind
of people you call us to be. May the community look
at our buildings and at us, and may there be a
Christ-likeness to see.

Amen.

Sundogs and Other Signs

When the bow is in the clouds, I will see it and remember the everlasting covenant between God and every living creature of all flesh that is on the earth.

(Genesis 9:16)

I had never seen a sundog until I moved to the Dakotas. In fact, I had never heard of the term *sundog* until I was living here in Fargo.

For those of you who are unfamiliar with the term, a *sundog* is kind of like a rainbow. It is a prism of beautiful colors of light that often surrounds the rising sun on a cold and dry morning. Sundogs are formed by the ice crystals in the cold air, and they refract the sunlight to form a kind of circular rainbow or halo of color around the sun.

On a really cold, clear morning, a sundog will often appear before the sun actually breaks the horizon—bringing with it a beautiful promise of a sunny, cold, and clear day. Some days the sundog will follow the rising sun most of the early morning hours. On a really cold, clear day, there may even be two or more sundogs refracting a beautiful prism of light around the rising sun.

Much like rainbows, sundogs appear as a prom-

---

ise of better weather to come. Rainbows often appear after a heavy rainstorm, and the colors of the rainbow bring a promise of clearer weather. In much the same way, sundogs appear to promise a clear (but still cold) day, sometimes after several days of winter storms.

In the Old Testament story of the great flood, God told Noah that the rainbow would be a reminder of God's covenant and God's promise not to allow the world to be destroyed by flood again. So the rainbow—and maybe the sundog—are reminders of God's faithfulness to humankind.

We need those reminders today. Too often we think that our religious activity is the basis of our faith, that our goodness is what qualifies us for life as a disciple of Christ. Too often we act as if God depends upon us to make the world a better place.

Rainbows and sundogs remind us that our faith is based upon God's covenant with us—a covenant that is unbreakable. We may rebel against God, we may break ourselves against God's laws, but we never break God's covenant. God promises that God's love and grace will always be with us, in spite of our own human frailty.

I am so glad that my Christian faith does not depend upon my understanding, my goodness, or my faithfulness. No, my faith is based upon God's promises and God's covenant with us. I may fail (and I often do), but God does not fail.

A few years ago, I heard a true story about a college football place kicker who missed the potential game-winning field goal at the end of the last big game of the season. The kicker was disconsolate over his failure, and there was nothing his teammates or coaches could do to help him feel better. Finally the head coach simply said to him, "You missed the kick, but the sun will still come up in the morning." The next morning at 6:30 A.M., the kicker received a phone call from the coach. He simply said, "Look out the window. The sun did rise today."

The next season, that same kicker went on to have a "perfect season"—hitting every field goal and every point-after-touchdown. He practiced hard all summer, and he improved his kicking technique. But I believe his improvement was also due to the reminder of his coach, "You missed the kick, but the sun will still come up in the morning."

It helps to keep things in perspective. Every rainbow and every sundog remind us, "Yes, you are human and you often fail to live up to God's standards. But God's covenant is eternal, and God loves you nonetheless and not the less."

And so I pray:

O LORD,
Thank you for sundogs and other signs
That remind us of your faithful love.
Thank you, Lord, for rainbows and other signs
Of your faithfulness from above.

All of us are so human, all of us are so filled
With errors and with failures, too.
Keep on reminding us, O Lord,
That our faith really depends upon you.

Every colorful sundog and beautiful sunrise
Comes to us with beauty in the morning hour,
To remind us that our trust is always misplaced,
Unless we place our faith in your great power.
                                                    AMEN.

THE PRISONER'S MITE

[Jesus] sat down opposite the treasury, and watched the crowd putting money into the treasury. Many rich people put in large sums. A poor widow came and put in two small copper coins, which are worth a penny. Then he called his disciples and said to them, "Truly I tell you, this poor widow has put in more than all those who are contributing to the treasury. For all of them have contributed out of their abundance, but she out of her poverty has put in everything she had, all she had to live on."

(Mark 12:41-44)

Over my years of ministry I have known many generous givers. Some gave their time, some gave their money, and some gave other gifts. Some of those generous persons were rather rich, and they gave very large gifts. Some were rather poor, and their gifts were small but sacrificial. We read in Scripture that Jesus commended one poor widow for giving the "widow's mite"—a small coin that represented a very large sacrifice on her part. Most recently I have learned about the gift of a group of prisoners in South Dakota that I call "The Prisoner's Mite."

Our United Methodist church in McCook Lake has arranged for four prisoners from the state prison in Springfield, South Dakota, to help with the renovation of their church facility. This is part of a program of the state to allow prisoners who are trustworthy to leave the prison each day and to work for nonprofit groups, with each prisoner being paid twenty-five cents per hour for this work. Of course part of the benefit to those prisoners is being able to leave the prison each day, to work on the "outside," and to experience some freedom briefly.

This program requires quite a commitment from our folks at McCook Lake. Each day someone must pick up the prisoners, take responsibility for them, feed them their meals, and return them each evening to the prison. It has also been a great benefit to our church, since these four men have construction skills that are needed. This process has also required some patience from everyone, since these prisoners are laboring right alongside the church volunteers who are working on the project.

All four of the prisoners have been so impressed by the way the church people have treated them ("like we are real human beings" according to one prisoner), that the four prisoners have decided to donate all of the money they are being paid by the state for their work. Now, twenty-five cents per hour is not much money, but for those four prisoners, it is all that they have.

One of the prisoners is being released on parole soon. One of the men from the church has agreed to give him a spare bedroom in his own house, in exchange for his continued work on the church project. He plans to attend church at McCook Lake United Methodist Church, too, and I am sure that he will be a blessing to that congregation even as they are a blessing to him.

So, this is a story about giving—giving humane treatment to people who are paying for their previous mistakes, giving an ex-con a second chance to make it on the "outside," giving a church help with their construction and renovation project, and giving the "prisoner's mite" to help with the costs. As I re-read the story of the widow's mite, somehow I know that Jesus is also pleased with all these gifts.

And so I pray:

O LORD,
You call us to be givers, those who freely give;
People who know they have been blessed to receive;
People who are ready to share with one another;
People who give like they say they believe.

It seems to me that stinginess is one of the ways
That we limit our faith and avoid spiritual growth;
When we are reluctant to share and to trust,
We are violating our faith and our Christian oath.

So, help us to know how deeply we have received
From the bounty of your goodness and your grace.
Then help us to be generous, gracious, and giving
To reflect to one another your smiling face.

AMEN.

PRAYED FOR

We have not ceased praying for you and asking that you may be filled with the knowledge of God's will in all spiritual wisdom and understanding.   (Colossians 1:9)

I am seldom speechless, at least not for long; but I recently had an experience that left me nearly without words. It occurred in the middle of a worship service where I was to preach in one of our churches in the Dakotas. There was a time of greeting one another, and it included the usual warm conversation, handshaking, and a few hugs. In the midst of all that, a woman came up to me and said, "I just want you to know, Bishop, that I pray for you every day." I was so nearly speechless that I could only utter, "Thank you. I need prayers every day."

What a wonderful thing it is to know that you are prayed for! How precious it is to be held in prayer by persons without our even knowing. Indeed all of us need prayer every day, and it is encouraging to think that there are persons praying for us.

Often we overlook the power of that act of prayer. I hear lots of "joys and concerns" in our congregational worship, followed by a pastoral prayer, silent prayer, and perhaps the Lord's Prayer shared together. I

---

know that lots of our churches have prayer chains—
groups of persons who commit to pray for any prayer
requests. I am aware of some churches that have
mid-week prayer services or prayer groups.
Sometimes all of that can seem routine or even mundane. Do we know the power of prayer, and do we
know the power of being prayed for?

Prayer is the act of centering upon God's presence in order to discover and to obey God's will. In
the Hebrew language of the Old Testament, God's
"presence" and God's "will" are the same basic
word. When we enter into God's presence through
prayer, it is our attempt also to follow God's will.

Prayer is not our effort to inform God, to bend
God's will to our needs, or to tell God what God
should be doing. Prayer is our effort to discover
God's will and to enter into it. Our model for prayer
is that of Jesus in the Garden of Gethsemane, who
anguished over his fate on the cross, but who ultimately prayed, "Thy will be done."

So, when we are prayed for, people are actually
praying that God's will and God's presence may
become real in our lives, and that we can respond
to God's presence and obey God's will.

It is a powerful thing to pray for others, and it is
a powerful thing to be prayed for. It's like an experience I remember with my son (now a young adult)
when he was only four or five. We walked by an
electric substation that had a huge warning sign,
"Danger! High Voltage." In my fatherly way I tried to
explain to Steve what that sign meant, and I asked
him, "Do you understand that?" He responded with
childlike honesty by saying, "Yes, it means don't
mess with this!"

Prayer is not something to "mess with" or to take
lightly. Perhaps one of the least helpful things we

do to one another in the church is to glibly say, "I will pray for you." Prayer is serious, powerful, wonderful, mysterious, and effective.

This is why I was so honored and blessed to be told, "Bishop, I pray for you every day." May we all pray for one another, and may our prayer always be, "Thy will be done."

And so I pray:

O LORD,
What a blessing it is to be able to pray, to have the opportunity to talk with you each day.

When I try to live my life on my own, under my own direction, I find that I am filled with pride, ego, and huge imperfection.

But you invite everyone one of us, including me, to prayerfully find what your will for us may be.

So, Lord, teach us to pray for ourselves and for each other; for this is what makes us your family, every sister and brother.

Thanks for those who pray for me each day, who prayerfully hope that I will follow faithfully your way.

Help our whole church to be a prayerful community for that will help us to maintain your perfect unity.
AMEN.

LOST AND FOUND

---

*When she has found it, she calls together her friends
and neighbors, saying, "Rejoice with me, for I have found
the coin that I had lost." Just so, I tell you, there is joy in
the presence of the angels of God over one sinner who
repents.* (Luke 15:9-10)

The fifteenth chapter of the Gospel of Luke
contains three parables of Jesus about the joy of
finding something that had been lost: a shepherd
found his lost sheep, a woman found her lost coin,
and a father found his lost son. Each of those parables focuses upon the utter joy of finding that
which had been lost. While we were traveling in
Israel, we saw a similar example of the joy of finding something that was lost. You might call this the
Parable of the Lost Passport.

It happened on our last night in Israel. Our bus
driver dropped our group off at a restaurant in the
new part of Jerusalem for our "last supper" before
heading to the airport in Tel Aviv to fly home.
Because of the heavy traffic in the area, our bus
driver told us that he would return at 8 P.M. to pick
us up. We went into the hotel for our meal, and my
administrative secretary, Naomi Bartle—the most
organized person in the entire world—suddenly
discovered that she had lost her passport!

Her discovery led to a frantic couple of hours while the Educational Opportunities people swung into action, calling the last sites we had visited, having people search the hotel where we had stayed in Jerusalem, calling the bus driver on his cell phone to see if her passport was on the bus (he could not find it), and making initial contacts to see about getting Naomi a replacement passport. For those two hours, it looked like we would have to leave Naomi in Israel, in order for her to go to the local police station to file a report, and then to go to the US Consulate in Jerusalem to get a replacement passport—all of which would take another day or two. Because her purse with the passport also contained her cash and credit card, she had no money, so our bus group quickly gathered over six hundred dollars to help with these extra expenses.

Our guide was very helpful and soothing, and I spent several phone calls with various Educational Opportunities people trying to find answers and making sure that they would take care of Naomi if we left her behind. All the while, Naomi remained relatively calm, but obviously concerned about having to stay behind in another country to try to get a new passport (she had made a photocopy of her passport that she kept in her luggage, so that would help her to prove her case—a good tip for anyone traveling to another country).

Finally we waited outside for our bus, hoping that Naomi might find she had simply dropped her passport somewhere on the bus. Our whole bus group (and the other bus group from the Dakotas that left ahead of us from the restaurant) was worried and concerned for Naomi. While we waited, we all talked about our trip and the many sites we had visited. One of our group asked me what had been the highlight of our trip to the Holy Land, and I replied hopefully, "It hasn't happened yet. My highlight is going to be when Naomi gets on that bus and finds her passport!"

The bus arrived, and we all waited while Naomi got on board first to look for her wallet and passport. Suddenly through the window we saw her joy as she found the wallet and held it up for all of us to see! Our entire group broke into a cheer on that street corner in Jerusalem, and I am sure that the entire city heard us. We got on board, hugged Naomi, praised God, and shared her joy (and relief). Once we got to the airport in Tel Aviv, we shared our good news with the other Dakotas bus group, and they also cheered and shouted until I thought that the Israeli security people might object to our behavior! It was a moment of sheer joy—what was lost had been found!

In Luke 15, Jesus makes it clear that our joy about finding anything lost is mirrored by the joy in heaven over anyone who repents and enters into the kingdom of God. The message seems clear: the kingdom of God is all about rejoicing for those who find God's way in their life! When the "lost" are "found" it is a cause for rejoicing!

How about those of us in the church? Do we share that joy? Do we rejoice over anyone who newly commits his or her life to Christ? Do we rejoice whenever a new member professes faith and joins our congregation? Do we celebrate with the person who reaches a milestone of sobriety? Do we share the joy of the drug addict who reforms, the convict who is released from prison, the abuser who stops abusing, the thief who quits stealing, the unbeliever who finally believes?

Or do we see our faith and church life as a reluctant duty? Do we begrudge those who finally reform from loose living? Do we complain about sending our money beyond our church walls in mission to others? Do we feel so self-righteous that we don't need God's forgiveness? Are we unable to rejoice with those who need and find God's grace?

The kingdom of God is about joy—the joy of the lost being found. And the message of the Parable of the Lost Passport is simply this: if we can rejoice over a found passport, imagine how much God rejoices over a found life.

And so I keep on rejoicing as I pray:

O GOD   ———————
Of the Lost and Found,
Keep on searching and waiting for us;
Don't give up on anyone,
But keep on loving and calling to us.

Help us to rejoice with you
Over any who are able to find your way;
Help us to rejoice with you
As others enter your kingdom today.

Your kingdom is about the joy
Of being lost and then being found;
We join with you in rejoicing
In your kingdom where grace abounds.

                                                  AMEN.

SPIRITUAL?

By contrast, the fruit of the Spirit is love, joy, peace, patience, kindness, generosity, faithfulness, gentleness, and self-control. There is no law against such things.

(Galatians 5:22-23)

A recent article in *USA Today* contained this quotation from David Kinnaman, "Spirituality in the U.S. is a mile wide and an inch deep." I think he is right.

Today the word *spiritual* has become a popular term that seems to be losing its meaning. Nearly everything is called spiritual and nearly every belief or religion seems to make its claim to the word. Even in the life of the church we seem to be rather mushy with our use of this word. I hear people say that they want their pastor to be more spiritual, or they want their worship service to be more spiritual, or they even want the annual conference session to be more "spiritual." Certainly there is nothing wrong with those desires, and certainly the church and its ministry should have a spiritual dimension.

But the word *spiritual* also leads to a lot of confusion. No one can argue against the desire for the church and its ministry to be more spiritual, but few seem to have any real content to their use of that word. Oftentimes the use of the word *spiritual* is really a disguise for someone's preference of style (what is spiritual in a worship service for some is not for someone else). Some even use the word *spiritual* as a weapon—they can always accuse the church or some pastor or some layperson of not being "spiritual enough," and who can defend oneself against such a charge?

I think that article in *USA Today* is right on target. For too many people in the US (and in our churches today), their sense of spirituality is a "mile wide and an inch deep."

Perhaps it would help us United Methodists, at least, to turn to our Wesley Quadrilateral of Scripture, tradition, reason, and experience whenever we talk about things spiritual. We might be reminded that seeking to be "spiritual" is not enough, unless it is linked to the Holy Spirit, the Spirit of Christ, and growing into the spiritual likeness of Christ. We might want to remember that the Scriptures remind us to test the spirits and not to be misled into believing that everything that claims to be "spiritual" is really of God. The primary test of the Spirit is the fruit of the Spirit in Galatians 5: Does the one who claims to be "spiritual" show the fruit of love, joy, peace, patience, goodness, gentleness, and self-control? We also might learn from our church traditions some of the real content to the word *spiritual,* and thus learn not to use the word so glibly.

I am delighted that people in the US and in our churches have a yearning for spiritual realities. I believe God is at work in this yearning and that people are seeking the spiritual realities of God, whether they know that or not. And I believe that The United Methodist Church must always seek to grow into the spiritual likeness of Christ. However, I believe that the guidance of things like our Wesley Quadrilateral is needed lest we fall into the trap of just mimicking the latest fad of our culture to seek anything that claims to be "spiritual."

All around the Dakotas I see examples of "spiritual" life that are not just fads or easy platitudes. I see people giving their time, their monetary gifts, and their talents to meet the needs of the churches and communities. As I visit our churches I hear our people praying faithfully for one another, for the sick and the hurting, and for the whole world. I watch pastors render ministry day in and day out, often without notice or much reward. I see reports of churches that pay their conference apportionments, not because it is a "tax" or even a duty, but because they want to share in extending their ministry beyond their own communities. I read newsletters and hear about programs and projects in our churches that teach God's Word, that care about children, that minister to the youth and to the aged, and that promote God's work and mission. And I meet wonderful people everywhere I go, people whose lives and witness display a depth of Spirit and a faithfulness to God that is inspiring.

Most of these examples of "spiritual" behavior happen without fanfare or any claim of spiritual superiority. Most will never catch the attention of their local papers, let alone *USA Today*. Most will not even be appreciated, except by those who benefit from their generosity and faithfulness. But somehow I know that God is pleased by the spiritual fruit in the lives of God's faithful people. And that is the best definition of *spiritual* that I know.

And so I pray:

O LORD,
Make us more spiritual, if that is your desire,
And let our spirits grow and glow with your heavenly fire.

But save us from the cheap, the petty, and the boasting fate
Of having a spirituality that is only second-rate.

May our churches grow in the likeness of Christ and in his Spirit,
Until our witness is strong and genuine to all who can hear it.

Thank you for the test of the Spirit that you gave us.
May those fruitful results be measured by your grace that saves us.

AMEN.

GETTING THE
FAMILY TOGETHER

Now you are the body of Christ and individually members of it   *(1 Corinthians 12:27)*

---

*A*s I write this message I am in Atlanta attending the Seventh Consultation of Methodist Bishops, a gathering of bishops from The United Methodist Church, the Christian Methodist Episcopal Church (CME), the African Methodist Episcopal Church (AME), and the African Methodist Episcopal Zion Church (AMEZ). In many ways it is like a family reunion among Methodist leaders.

Our Methodist family in America is broken because of racism. When the Methodist Episcopal Church (ME) was established in America in 1784, it contained European American and African American members. Because of their experiences of racism in that new church, many African Americans left in 1816 to form the AME Church and another group left in 1821 to form the AMEZ Church. After the ME Church itself split over slavery in 1844, another split occurred in 1870 when many African American members left the Methodist Episcopal Church South to form the Colored Methodist Episcopal Church, which later changed its name to the Christian Methodist Episcopal Church.

The reuniting of The Methodist Church in 1939 and the subsequent 1968 merger with the Evangelical United Brethren did not include the AME, AMEZ, or CME churches. Still today, these predominantly African American Methodist denominations are separate from one another and from The United Methodist Church (UMC). Racism still splits the US Methodist family.

Starting in 1979, the bishops of our four Methodist denominations have held consultations every four years to talk about shared ministries, cooperation, better understanding, and even union. These consultations have provided a time for the leaders of our Methodist family to gather.

This consultation (my first) began with a dynamic worship service, and it has continued with scholarly presentations, small group discussions, announcements of shared programs, and time to build relationships among the bishops of our Methodist family. Out of this experience, I share the following observations:

• Racism is real and contemporary. The issue of "white privilege" continues to be harmful in our society and in our Methodist family.
• Seeing and hearing how our divisions from the 1800's continue to haunt us reminds me that we in The United Methodist Church should never speak lightly of splits today. Although some grow impatient with current problematic issues, our previous divisions should teach us that church schism is always painful and long-term.

- Reconciliation is possible, but it requires dialogue, mutual understanding, and acts of confession/repentance on all sides. No one can remove the pain of the past, but God's grace does allow us to make a fresh start with one another as brothers and sisters.
- We need each other. Whether we actually merge our denominations or just learn to cooperate better, we need the gifts, history, and personality that are brought to the reunion by every member of the family.

The issues of this consultation may seem quite distant from the Dakotas, since there are no AME, CEM, or AMEZ churches in either state. However, we in the Dakotas also face the evil of racism as it applies to attitudes toward Native Americans, jealousies among various European American groups, and our blindness toward emerging ethnic groups in the Dakotas, such as our increasing Hispanic population.

The sin of racism plagues us all, even if its forms in the Dakotas are different from those being discussed here at the Consultation of Methodist Bishops. I long and I pray for the day when all of God's children will see and accept each other's differences and each other's gifts. Maybe it will only happen in the kingdom of God, but I pray for that reality to be present soon.

And so I pray:

O LORD,

Draw us together as one large family. Help us to see and to know our sisters and brothers. For all of us who are human are your kin, and we must learn how to live in peace with one another.

Our Methodist family is still split and divided, still hurt by pains and divisions from long ago. Only your grace and your love can heal us and save us from earthly divisions here below.

Give us a vision of your family, O God. Help us to see that all upon this earth are our kin. Lead us to love and to accept one another, and to restore the unity of your family once again.

AMEN.

TURBULENCE

And not only that, but we also boast in our sufferings, knowing that suffering produces endurance, and endurance produces character, and character produces hope, and hope does not disappoint us, because God's love has been poured into our hearts through the Holy Spirit that has been given to us. (Romans 5:3-5)

---

*I*t was 5:30 A.M., and I was sitting on a plane at the Fargo airport waiting to fly to a meeting in New York. Even though I was sleepy, I could overhear the flight attendants talking with the pilot and copilot. Evidently their landing the previous night in Fargo had been quite turbulent, due to the high winds and driving rainstorm of that evening. One of the flight attendants asked, "Will there be any turbulence today?" The pilot responded, "Not until we take off."

That pilot was speaking the truth about life, not just about flying an airplane. Turbulence only comes from being in flight, being on the move, going somewhere. Oh yes, there are sometimes windy conditions on the ground while we hunker down seeking safety. But turbulence—real turbulence—only comes when we are on the move.

Sometimes in the church and in our ministry we feel that turbulence. Sometimes when we take a stand, when we deal with difficult issues, when we hold people accountable, or when we start making the changes that may lead to effective ministry—sometimes that is when we feel the most "turbulence" in the church. People may start to resist change, feel uncomfortable as the church moves into the future, and begin to complain. Some people will say, "I wish things could be like they used to be." Others will say, "This is not the same church it used to be."

In the Old Testament we read the story of the Israelite people in the Sinai Desert after the Exodus from Egypt. Although Moses had led the people to freedom from their slavery to Pharaoh, it didn't take long for people to begin to complain. Some even formed the "Back to Egypt Committee" to say, "Weren't we better off when we were slaves?" Moses felt the turbulence. His own sister led a rebellion against his leadership. His brother Aaron gave the people the comfort that they wanted: a golden calf so they could worship the safe, familiar gods from Egypt. And Moses often wondered why God had called him to lead such a people.

In the ministry of Jesus in the New Testament, we read in the Gospel of John about a time when the great crowds began to fade and to fall away from Jesus. Jesus felt the turbulence and asked his remaining few disciples, "Do you also wish to go away?" (John 6:67).

Turbulence, resistance, complaints, uneasiness, fear of the future, discomfort with change: All of these elements can occur when our churches and our ministry begin to take off. In fact, it is one of the most surprising aspects of ministry—that many people complain and cause turbulence just when the church begins to make progress, when new members are starting to join, when the worship attendance is increasing, and when the ministry seems to be making a difference in people's lives. It is then, when things are starting to happen, that turbulence is most likely to come.

Now, we must be careful and not assume that turbulence means that we are "right" and others are "wrong." As someone has said, "Just because the people want to stone me, that doesn't make me a prophet." Sometimes the criticism, the fear, and uneasiness are due to honest differences and to valuable critiques.

However, it is most often true that the turbulence comes from our fear of change, even good change. Recently one layperson wrote to me to complain about all of the changes and new ministries that are happening in her church. She said, "I know we are doing better financially, and I see lots of new members joining, and I sense a much better spirit in our congregation; but I am afraid that all of these changes won't last and that our church will be disappointed again."

She was describing the most insidious form of turbulence, the fear of succeeding. You see, for some people (remember those Israelites in the desert) failure has become so comfortable that success feels like a threat to our status quo. Some people prefer to return to slavery in Egypt rather than to face the frightening consequences of freedom and new opportunities.

I have seen it happen. I have seen individuals who start to get their lives straightened out, then they fall back into old, destructive habits because that feels "familiar" and less threatening. I have seen churches that have pulled back from effective ministry just as they were starting to accomplish something, because it was more comfortable to deal with failure and guilt. I have seen pastors who just could not seem to give themselves permission to do well in ministry, so that each time they began to succeed they would do something stupid to get themselves in trouble again.

There isn't much turbulence sitting on the ground, playing it safe. Let's face the turbulence head on, let's provide comfort to those who fear flying; but let's not just taxi around and pretend that we are flying. Remember: There isn't any turbulence until we take off.

And so I pray:

O Lord,
Help us when the turbulence comes,
When our discipleship and faithfulness might wane;
Show us that following you is not always easy,
But neither is following you ever in vain.

Help our church be alive and vital and moving,
Help us to get our ministries off of the ground;
Give us strength to follow your leading through change
So that your grace may also be found.

Help us face the turbulence with faith and strength,
Never becoming deterred from our task;
Your presence in the midst of the windstorms
Is all that we need or dare to ask.

Amen.

LOOKING THROUGH
THE WINDSHIELD

---

*F*or now we see in a mirror, dimly, but then we will see
face to face.   (1 Corinthians 13:12)

---

*I*t was bound to happen. With all the miles I
drive here in the Dakotas, and with all of the rocks
and debris that are flipped on my car by passing
trucks, it was just a matter of time. Finally it happened on I-29 north of Sioux Falls, as I was traveling about 75 mph. A rock flipped up from the road-
way and cracked my windshield. At first it was just
a tiny little crack, but as I continued on that journey over the next few days the crack grew larger
and larger. It was kind of interesting to watch it
slowly expand, and it formed some interesting geo-
metric shapes. A couple of times I even found
myself looking so closely at the crack in my windshield that I wasn't carefully observing the road
ahead.

So of course I had to get the whole windshield
replaced, and what a difference it made! It wasn't
merely that the new windshield was no longer
cracked; now I had a whole, new, and very clear,
view of the world. Since the old windshield had
been with me for 102,000 miles, it was more pitted

---

and hazy than I had realized. The new windshield gave me a refreshing view of the world and of the road I was traveling. It was great to be able to see clearly again!

Sometimes we discover that we have been traveling through life with impaired vision. Sometimes we have gotten so used to "seeing through a glass darkly" (as Paul puts it) that we do not realize our vision is only partial. Sometimes we more readily see the cracks and the problems that are just in front of our nose, and we aren't really looking at the whole vista in front of us.

Sometimes it is even worse than that. Dr. Doug Anderson, who is the executive director of the Bishop Rueben Job Center for Leadership Development here in the Dakotas, says that often church leaders think they are looking through the windshield, when actually they are looking into the rear-view mirror! As Doug says, it is very difficult to drive a car by looking only in the rear-view mirror. We need to be sure that we are looking through the windshield to see what it ahead of us.

How about you? Are you looking through a glass that is cracked, dark, pitted, and distorted? Are you focusing too closely upon the problems that are close at hand, so that you cannot see the whole panorama of God's world? Are you looking into a rear-view mirror, trying to find the future by only viewing the past?

How about your church? Is your vision focused too closely upon small problems that you face? Is your vision for the future impaired by too much attachment to "the ways we used to do things"? Is your vision limited by problems and distortions that you aren't even aware of?

It has always intrigued me that Jesus taught in

parables and then said, "Let anyone with ears to hear listen." He might have said, "Let anyone with eyes to see have vision." He seemed to imply that everything about God's will is not always obvious or easy. We need to be open, ready, available, perceptive, and risking in order to discover God's way in our lives.

Only God can help us raise our eyes beyond any current horizon in order to see the full majesty of God's creation and God's purpose in our lives. Only God can grant us the discernment to see and to perceive God's truth. Only God can help us perceive with eyes of faith.

Vision for ministry and for meaning in life comes from God. But sometimes it helps to get a new windshield—or at least to make sure we aren't looking into the rear-view mirror.

And so I pray:

O LORD,
I want to see clearly, I want to know your ways.
Lord, I want to perceive your truth and to follow you always.

Give me eyes that can see, ears that can hear your voice, wisdom to truly perceive, courage to make the right choice.

Lord, I want your church to see clearly. I want all of us to know your ways. Lord, I want us to perceive your truth and to follow you always.
                                                              AMEN.

LESSONS FROM A KILDEER

Jerusalem, Jerusalem, the city that kills the prophets and stones those who are sent to it! How often have I desired to gather your children together as a hen gathers her brood under her wings, and you were not willing!

(Luke 13:34)

*W*ork has finally begun on the new parking lot behind my office here in Fargo. We moved the area office into an office wing constructed for us in the new Friendship United Methodist Church, and we have been waiting for the completion of the parking lot.

Just before the big machines arrived to turn the earth, pack the earth, and prepare the base for the parking lot, a small mother killdeer evidently prepared a nest in the grass and laid three eggs. Although her nest is up near the building and relatively safe, she has been very upset by the arrival of all these workmen and huge pieces of machinery. Every day she squawks at the workmen, runs around on the ground feigning an injured wing to draw them away from her nest, and does everything she can to protect her soon-to-be-hatched babies.

The children in the daycare center here at the

church have placed a small flag near the nest, just to remind the workmen to be careful and to avoid hitting it. But really their flag is not necessary, because that mother bird will NOT allow anyone or anything get near her nest. Her fierce, brave, protective love is amazing!

I am reminded that the Bible is full of images of God as "father," but the Bible also has many images of God as a "mother." The word that Jesus used to name God, *Abba*, is actually an Aramaic word that little children used to call either their mommy or their daddy. It is the word of a child toward a loving and protective parent.

Lately the British Methodist Church has stirred up a huge controversy by including in their new worship book a prayer that says, "God our Father and our Mother, we give you thanks and praise." Many people, even in the secular press, are greatly distressed that anyone would consider addressing God has "Mother."

Somehow we have missed the point. God is not male or female. God is God. All of our human efforts to name God are inadequate. But this we do know: God is a like a loving, protective parent to us. It is certainly appropriate to claim all of the best of fatherhood for our understanding of God. It is appropriate to call God "Father" so long as we do not limit God by that title.

It is also appropriate to use "mothering" images for God's love for us. Jesus himself cried over Jerusalem with these words, "How often have I desired to gather your children together as a hen gathers her brood under her wings, and you were not willing!" (Luke 13:34). God is beyond our human expressions, our human names, and even our human relationships; but it is always appropriate to learn from the best of our human relationships and to apply those lessons to our relationship with God. That's why I have learned a lot about God's protective, parenting love for all of us by watching a little mother bird protect her nest. How much does God love us? Learn from a mother killdeer.

And so I pray:

O GOD,
You are more than Father or Mother to us,
You are our heavenly Creator and Parent;
All of our words are inadequate to describe
Your love for us, which is so apparent.

Like a loving father who cares for us deeply,
Like a mother bird protecting her little nest;
Your love for us can never be explained,
But your love compares to the loves we know best.

So help us to learn from all those who love,
Help us to learn to be loving just like you;
Please God, keep on loving and protecting us,
Just like a mother bird seems to know how to do.
                                        AMEN.

O CANADA!

As he walked by the Sea of Galilee, he saw two brothers,
Simon, who is called Peter, and Andrew his brother, cast-
ing a net into the sea—for they were fishermen. And he
said to them, "Follow me, and I will make you fish for peo-
ple." Immediately they left their nets and followed him.

(Matthew 4:18-20)

Early this summer my wife and I joined several people on a retreat and fishing trip to Canada. We enjoyed the hospitality of Norm Neumann, one of our Dakotas Conference retired pastors, whose cabin is located on the Winnipeg River. In order to get to Norm's cabin, one drives six-and-a-half hours north of Fargo (yes, for those of you outside of the Dakotas, there is that much of the earth north of Fargo—there is a whole country up there!); then Norm meets you at the marina and takes you by boat the two-and-a-half miles upriver to his cabin. It is remote, and it is beautiful country. The river is wide and smooth; pine trees are all around; dozens of eagles, lots of deer, bears, and other wildlife share the remoteness. And of course there are fish to be caught.

Fishing for walleye is fun. I am not much of a fisher person, but I enjoyed the setting, the company, and the fishing experience. I will share my novice fishing experience and make a not-too-subtle comparison to the "fishing for people" that Christ calls us to as a church:

• Fishing requires a lot of patience. The fish don't just jump on the hook or lure because we go out in a boat and look for them. It takes patience, the right timing, and lots of effort.

• Fishing requires going to the right spot. Often you have to move from spot to spot in order to find the place where the fish are most receptive to your fishing efforts.

• Fishing requires the proper equipment. Some of those on our trip took enough equipment to fish for a decade, but they were prepared! As Bill Bates said at one point on our trip, "When the fish are biting, it helps to have extra rods all prepared, because you don't want to waste time repairing a rod and miss the opportunity."

• Fishing requires skill, and that skill improves with practice. My early attempts at casting (as we fished for northern) were not nearly as effective as my later attempts. Practice, and learning from someone who knows how to fish, improves one's ability to fish.

• Fishing is worth it. All of that effort, patience, practice, and skill come together in a wonderful moment of enjoying a fresh fish dinner with friends on a cool Canadian evening.

Do I really have to make the parallels to the task of evangelism for the church? Jesus told

Simon, Andrew, James, and John, "Follow me, and I will make you fish for people." We in the church are still learning how to "fish" for new people to the faith. We often forget that skill, patience, practice, new techniques, and appropriate opportunities must come together for the right results.

Is it worth it? Yes! To help another person discover the good news of the gospel, to become a part of the fellowship and life of Christ's body in the church, and to grow in grace by the Holy Spirit—that is a wonderful thing to experience. It is almost as good as fishing in Canada.

So, keep trying new equipment, keep moving to new spots in the culture where people are more receptive, enjoy the fellowship as you fish together, share a few fish stories to encourage one another, and celebrate the results. Good fishing!

And so I pray:

———

O LORD,
Help us to fish well for men and women,
Help us to invite, welcome, and respond;
Help us to focus upon our evangelism,
Just like fishing in a river, lake, or pond.

Fishing for people is what we are called to do,
Fishing for people is what the church needs, too.

So, help us to be good fishers of people,
Help us to enjoy reaching out to others.
Let us be a church that "fishes" for folks,
And welcomes them as sisters and brothers.
AMEN.

———

FINDING FAITH

———

Therefore, since we are surrounded by so great a cloud of witnesses, let us also lay aside every weight and the sin that clings so closely, and let us run with perseverance the race that is set before us, looking to Jesus the pioneer and perfecter of our faith, who for the sake of the joy that was set before him endured the cross, disregarding its shame, and has taken his seat at the right hand of the throne of God.

(Hebrews 12:1-2)

———

It was a Sunday evening. I had preached at our United Methodist church in Faith, South Dakota, that morning (along with Marcus Presbyterian, their sister church on the charge). I had conducted a ground-breaking service for a new church facility in Sturgis (in the midst of a downpour of rain), I had met with a prospective pastor from another denomination who would like to serve here in our conference, and I had met with the Pastor-Parish Relations Committee at Belle Fourche to hear more about their needs for a new pastor. Now it was time to drive back to Faith to rejoin my wife, who had remained behind to enjoy an afternoon of horseback riding on a lovely ranch.

———

I started east on US Highway 212 and, after passing through Newell, encountered a sign that warned, "No services the next 72 miles." Thus began the trip across the most remote part of South Dakota, where there was no sign of civilization for the next hour or so. I passed only three cars on the road, but there were so many bugs plastering my windshield in the twilight that I thought I would have to stop and use my ice scraper to clear a spot to see!

As the darkness descended, I hurried to find my way to Faith while there was still some light. I could only imagine how remote and dangerous that road might be in the midst of a winter snowstorm. Finding Faith, South Dakota, was a real relief after a long day and those desolate final miles.

Now, lest I get too sentimental, I should admit that Faith, is not named for any religious experience. The railroad owner named the four stops in that area after his four children: Marcus, Faith, Maurine, and Isabel. So Faith in South Dakota is not really a religious name, but finding Faith late at night after a long journey can be an almost religious experience. It was good to arrive at Faith and to enjoy more of the hospitality of the pastor, Muriel Oates, her husband Jim, and the lovely community.

My trip that night reminded me of another time that I truly traveled on faith. It was several years ago in Indiana. I had invited my colleague and friend, Ralph Karstedt, to preach at a mid-week service at my church in South Bend. While I was driving Ralph to Epworth Forest (one of our campgrounds), Ralph suggested taking the back roads, and he offered to navigate. That all sounds fine, unless you know that Ralph is blind. So there I was, driving late at night across the back roads of northern Indiana, guided by a blind pastor who knew the way from experience. He would say things like, "Now there should be a big red barn at the next crossroads, and that is where you turn left down a gravel road." Sure enough, Ralph was an excellent guide, and we arrived safely at our destination.

I often remember that journey by faith. Many times in life when the darkness is descending, the light is fading, we have to trust those who have gone before us to lead us safely home. That is what it means to travel by faith. Ralph has written an excellent book, *As I See It,* which describes his life as a United Methodist pastor who happens to be blind. Ralph's faith is obvious in that book. He talks a lot about what it is like to have to trust others to help him travel and minister.

The Letter to the Hebrews reminds us that Jesus Christ is our Pathfinder, the one who has traveled all of the hazards of life's journey—all the way to the cross—and he is the one who leads us by faith. Even when our guide seems blind. Even when the road has no services. Even when it seems we will never get to Faith. Still, Christ leads us home.

And so I pray:

O LORD,
Help us to travel by faith through these days,
Teach us how to be centered in your ways.

Guide us, direct us, and show us your high way,
Help us to avoid any detours or by-ways.

By faith we must travel wherever you lead,
Faith is the only way we can proceed.

AMEN.